P9-BYZ-864

Charles M. Olsen

Transforming Church Boards

into communities of spiritual leaders

An Alban Institute Publication

Copyright © 1995 by the Alban Institute, Inc. All rights reserved. Reprinted 1996, 1998, and 2000.

This material may not be photocopied or reproduced in any way without written permission.

Library of Congress Catalog Card Number 95-75680
ISBN 1-56699-148-X

CONTENTS

How to Read and Use this Book

If you want to understand what life on a "transformed" board is all about, you can experience it by reading this book. Dr. Arlo Duba, a trusted colleague, said to me, "Chuck, why don't you present the content and theory of your model in such a way as to allow the inquirer to experience it while reading?" That is what I have attempted to do.

I will tell you a story, lay a "master story" from the biblical tradition alongside it, then weave them together until a pattern of "distilled wisdom" emerges. After that we will "discern" how this wisdom works in board and council development and what visions it might project for a board's future. Suggestions for practical implementation cap off each chapter. The movement is labeled in each chapter, so you can't miss it. And the process is visualized in the following chart.

A Biblical/Theological Reflection Process

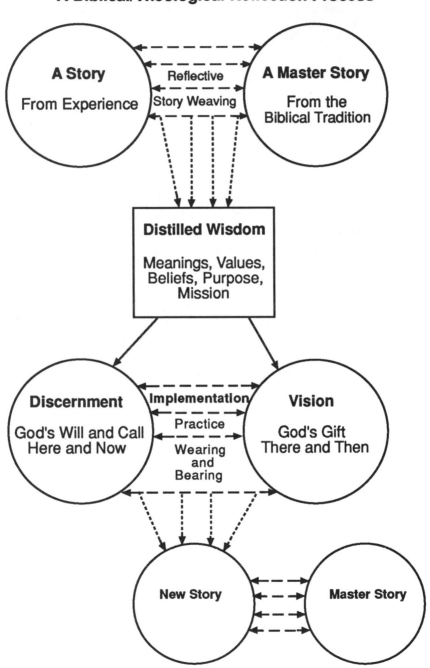

With Appreciation

To my wife, Joyce, who covered many bases in our home, office, and conference center—freeing and encouraging me to give time and attention to the writing of this book.

To Chuck Hamner, a friend of many years, who brought his editing skills and wisdom as a Presbyterian elder to the final shaping of the manuscript.

To Arlo Duba and Peter Morgan, whose critical reading and helpful suggestions resulted in the inclusion of stories and anecdotes.

To the Heartland Presbyterian Center—its board and staff and director, James Rhaesa—which has hosted the ecumenical project along with Heartland Presbytery.

To the many pastors and board/council members who have dreamed, striven, and struggled to follow a new way of "doing board." They are valued colleagues in this learning effort.

To my father, Melvin, who was elected an elder for life while still in his thirties—before the rotary term system was instituted—and who modeled eldership for me. And to my wife, mother, sisters, brother, and son—all of whom have been ordained as Presbyterian elders.

To Lilly Endowment, the financial support of which has made possible the gathering of an incredible array of talented people; and to Dr. James P. Wind, Lilly's project coordinator, who has been a perceptive questioner and encourager.

To the Spirit of God, who continues to make all things new.

INTRODUCTION

My time had come.

After participating in a clergy study-discussion group for nearly two years, it was my turn to present a discussion paper on a subject of my choosing. I had just returned from leading my congregation's annual board of elders' organizational retreat. I was still wrestling with the issues of lay leadership on church boards. But at a deeper level I wondered what was to become of the twelve officers we had just rotated off the board.

I had heard board members in my own and other churches say, "I'm glad it's almost over," or "Whew, I made it," or "Never again." What caused these negative feelings? I was especially dismayed at the number of former church officers who became inactive or even dropped out of the church.

So I wrote my discussion paper on the subject of what happens to former church officers and what their experience on a board may be doing to them. I was surprised but also intrigued by the strength of the group's reaction. Clearly, a nerve had been touched. An important but little-talked-about issue of congregational life had surfaced.

That was a defining moment for me, the catalyst for a series of events that have inexorably led me into a full-time calling to the study, development, and revitalization of church boards and councils.

My commitment to effective church boards was already long-standing. No matter what arena of ministry I have engaged in—whether as a pastor, a denominational staffer, or a project director—I have always functioned as a "renewalist." I hold a deep love for the church and a vision for its renewal. While pastoring three Presbyterian churches, I always invested deeply in a major agent of renewal, the session, the official board of elders.

In the midseventies I had pioneered an Atlanta-based project with the Institute for Church Renewal that specialized in establishing and nurturing new forms of Christian community in small groups and house churches. I told my wife, Joyce, when we were leaving the Atlanta project for a pastorate that some day—when the kids were educated and college bills were paid—I could see myself returning to a ministry in the church at large as "an apostle." I remembered that a Canadian Mennonite friend, John Miller, had observed that I demonstrated the gifts of "an apostle," one who travels around hearing and telling stories that encourage such fledgling groups.

In 1990 I realized that the time had come to follow a new calling. I was challenged in this calling by Fr. Joe Gremillion of Notre Dame, who said, "Chuck, lead and inspire a movement of renewal and revitalization of church boards across America."

Having directed Project Base Church, funded by the Lilly Endowment in the early 1970s, I returned to the endowment in 1990 with a vision and call to work for renewal in church boards through a project eventually named Set Apart Lay Leaders.

I learned that the Lilly Endowment had already been investing deeply in a series of efforts aimed at developing leadership on boards of trustees in the not-for-profit sector. These "trusteeship projects" were in keeping with the charge of Eli Lilly, an Episcopal layman who years ago set up the Lilly foundation to benefit education, religion, and community organizations, emphasizing leadership development within these arenas.

The endowment wanted to make a difference in the not-for-profit world; seeing the proliferation in American society of organizations governed by boards of trustees, it had decided to invest there. I came to Lilly saying I wanted to work exclusively with church boards.

There are 350,000 congregations in the United States, most of them with boards or councils. Some of these bodies, particularly the Roman Catholic parish councils, have a very short history—only about twenty-five years. If each board averages eight or nine people, there are three million church board members! Given the difficulties that many boards face and the lack of fulfillment that many board members experience, this seemed a ripe field for research and transformation.

The Lilly Endowment has been generous in its support of religious leadership development efforts in theological seminaries as well as in other training organizations. But no organization had focused its efforts on lay leadership of church boards. A move into church boards would wed Lilly's interest in trusteeship with leadership development and congregational studies. I received a one-year planning grant to "reconnoiter" the landscape of church governance to see what was and was not happening. Evaluations and learnings from the trusteeship projects were reviewed to see what might be translated for use by church boards and councils. In addition, I conducted nearly two hundred interviews with lay church officers, pastors, seminary administrators and faculty, denominational and judicatory staff members, and others who work in leadership and trustee development.

I heard a high level of frustration and even disillusionment among laypeople with their experience on church boards, much of it due to lack of a "missing" element—spirituality. New members expected that a church-board term would provide an opportunity to develop and deepen their faith. Too often they encountered "business as usual."

In response to what we heard, Set Apart Lay Leaders was designed as a three-year project that would develop and test strategies for integrating spirituality and administration in the meetings of boards.

The project was to glean the best insights from the world of not-for-profit trustee development but would do its theological homework so the model would be grounded in the gifts and resources of faith traditions. The project would be concerned with the selection and preparation of board members—but more. It would give attention to the integration of spirituality and administration at the board table so that meetings would be life giving rather than life draining. The board table was to become a locus for both individual and corporate spiritual formation.

The resultant model with its four practices—(1) history giving and story telling, (2) biblical-theological reflection, (3) prayerful discernment, and (4) "visioning" the future—was "planted" and tested in five covenant congregations.

We listed desired outcomes:

- Church officers will stay engaged in the life of the congregation when they rotate off of the board or council.
- The meetings will be energized with new vitality.
- Council members will grow in vitality and maturity of faith.
- Lay members on boards will develop a new capacity to theologize.
- Clergy will develop new enabling skills for board meetings.
- The laity will be empowered as they share ministry with clergy.

- The congregation will be affected by new ways of "doing board."
- The potential for conflict will be reduced.
- Corporate spirituality, as well as individual spirituality, will be recognized and valued.
- Incentives to serve on boards will be heightened.
- The climate for recruiting new board members will become more positive.
- The experience of serving on a church board or council will be seen as a training ground for "trusteeship" outside the church.

Within the first year, we added five additional churches to our core working group; these were intentional about the integration of spirituality and administration but working their own models (not our four-part model). We also selected five other congregational boards for baseline comparison. Trained interviewers then went into the fifteen churches—five covenant, five intentional, and five baseline—to glean their experience. Interviewers asked all boards the same set of questions:

- Tell us about your "yes" to serving on a church board.
- What was most fulfilling about your experience?
- What was "missing" for you?
- What do you actually do in your meetings?
- What has been the effect of what you do in meetings:
  (1) on your personal development? (2) on the life and vitality of the board? (3) on the congregation? (4) on your involvement in the wider community? (5) on the leadership capacities of the pastor?

The results of those interviews were presented to an annual collegium of people with interest in board development. The collegium concluded that the four-part model works and that all of the desired outcomes were present. We were making a significant difference in the transformation of church boards and councils!

The collegium also concluded that the model introduces a new paradigm for boards: *The individual board member is no longer seen as a political representative but as a spiritual leader. The board or council is no longer seen as a group of corporate managers, but as the people of God in community. The meeting is no longer seen as a litany of reports and decisions held together by "book-end" prayers but as "worshipful work."*

An advisory panel of nine members from a wide ecumenical span evaluated our efforts after one year. This advisory panel concluded that "the model is a transformational one which is tapping into a larger movement." The panel's report continued on a cautionary note:

> Concrete steps need to be taken to "nail down the movement so that it doesn't die in a muddle." When we deal with the culture of a church and board we will tap into both welcome and resistance. It may reduce conflict, but it may also stir things up!

The project continued to network with church leaders in many disciplines. The issues being addressed in the project continued to elicit a knowing yes from folks on the front lines of church administration.

When I named the malady of church boards the "D" word *(disillusionment)*, I learned to pause, for everyone had a story to tell! Paradoxically, two of the most frequent complaints were (1) "It's run just like a business" and (2) "It's not run enough like a business"! Both expressed dissatisfaction. One camp looked for efficiency models from business, while the other camp sought a whole different way of being board that would draw from the culture of faith communities.

When personal-experience stories come out, they often are couched in "something was missing" language. Having come to the board with an expectation that this would be a faith-deepening and faith-enhancing opportunity, new members found a "business as usual" board often bogged down in a time-consuming agenda. What was "missing" for them was a faith orientation.

We had learned much but had so much more to learn. We wanted to sharpen our definitions and deepen the practices in the model based on what we had learned in year one. We made some slight adjustments, then replanted it in sixteen additional covenanting churches of various sizes and denominations. As we moved toward the second collegium, we wrestled with a set of questions initiated by Craig Dykstra and Jim Wind at Lilly and by Shelby Andress at the Search Institute: (1) What is the desired change or preferred vision for the "culture" of boards/councils in congregations? (2) What does it take to change the culture of boards/councils and their members? How do they come to "get it"? (3) What does it take to catalyze that effort? (4) How can the catalyzing be done close at hand and from a distance? (5) What does it take to "make it stick," given turnover in membership and in pastoral and lay leadership?

To learn from the experiences of the covenanting churches, we sent trained observers to visit each board twice and record their observations. Their reports were summarized and presented to the second collegium. The observers reported that "story telling and history giving" is the easiest and most widely used piece of the model, and that "prayerful discernment" is the foggiest and least used.

The most gratifying outcome of the second collegium was unexpected: While the evaluator-respondents at the first collegium had posed the question, "Is the model complete and does it work?" the evaluator–respondents at the second collegium confidently asked, "How can the model be replicated and adapted for use in other settings?"

At the conclusion of our first year of working with five congregations and monitoring others for comparison, Set Apart Lay Leaders listed some learnings. We now know that:

- Although differing denominational traditions create special sets of governance circumstances, the issues that affect morale, motivation, and faith development are held in common.
- There is a widely perceived "hunger" in churches for ways to "do board differently." Many responses to the work of the Set Apart Lay Leaders project have come unsolicited from people who heard or read news releases about the project and instantly "connected" with it at a deep emotional and spiritual level.
- The model works. All the basic elements are present. Those churches that used it experienced a much higher level of life and vitality in meetings, along with less frustration, conflict, and gossip. Participants in the covenant churches reported increases in positive, open attitudes and three times the frequency in use of spiritual disciplines. References to an awareness of the presence of God and to their own personal faith development were mentioned twice as often as references by other church boards.
- The most satisfying aspect of service on boards was working closely and harmoniously together to accomplish meaningful work despite differences, diversity, or conflict.
- The model provided a language with which to talk about meetings and people's experience of them.

- "Corporate spirituality" is a foreign and uncomfortable concept. Personal spirituality is more palatable.
- There is tension between interpretive theory and practical how-to-do-it methods. We resist the danger of reducing the project to a "recipe," yet people see the process most clearly when they see models and examples. Experiencing the process in meetings is a way to "get it," with stories, face-to-face conversations, and biblical images helping to communicate it. To succeed the model must maintain a "simple elegance" and cannot become complicated. This spiritually oriented model needs to center on images of God and on scriptural texts images, and stories that provide "master stories" that both drive the model and interpret it.
- The language used needs to connect with participating lay-people. During the project's second year, *worshipful work* was embraced as a preferred vision for the spirit or culture of a board. This new self-definition powerfully shifts the paradigm for the board and its members.

One of the reactor-evaluators at the collegium, Mennonite historian Robert Kreider, commented in his report:

This is a countercultural enterprise. Here is a call to resist the seductive drag of modernity—individualism, competition, compartmentalization, specialization, secularization professionalization—to create community. And a special kind of community—a blessed community of praise, study, caring, discernment, and hope. Here is the vision of inviting the church council to become a nucleus for the renewal of the church. This is a radically different vision from a conventional acceptance of the church as hobby, one of a number of nice community activities. Church is serious business, not just an add-on.

This is a call for a shift in congregational power from the elite few to the noncredentialed many (the laity)—a shift, not a transfer or displacement. Here is a vision of every member a pastor, a serious Bible student, a student, and a teacher. This can be threatening as a power grab or supportive as power sharing. We are working with a concept of leadership as servanthood.

In calling the church council to be the church, one is working with yeasty stuff. If this integration of church housekeeping with worship and Bible study is good for the church council, then certainly this program vision would be salutary for every committee, task force, and board in the congregation: music, stewardship, day school, plant, youth, senior citizen program, etc. The effort to recover spiritual vitality in the church council could radiate out to permeate the entire congregation.

Acknowledging that our people are less and less literate biblically, this enterprise is a rigorous restoration motif: an intention to recover a broad-based biblical familiarity and seriousness, an effort to imprint in our minds, hearts, and lips the metaphors of Scripture. This is nothing less than a claim for biblical space alongside the language of sports, TV, the computer, and the marketplace.

As a "renewalist" I think strategically. For a time I worked to cultivate small groups alongside other traditional programs in the church because there we experienced life and vitality. But often those efforts were on the fringes of the program or membership. Now I am convinced that the most opportune place to exert influence for transformation is at the heart of the life of the church—the official board.

I see a future when boards function out of the heritage of a rich faith tradition rather than out of the latest fad in management circles.

- I see boards inspired and inspirational to the congregations they lead.
- I see people growing and healing and forming a deep faith at the tables of their meetings.
- I see meetings so alive that they seem shorter rather than longer than they actually are!
- I see congregations being transformed by the impetus their boards create.
- I see these rich board or council experiences moving across denominational lines so that Roman Catholic, mainline Protestant, evangelical Christian, and Jew can celebrate and learn from one another's stories.
- I see council members being schooled in an avenue of discipleship that will lead them into lay ministries in other board sectors —for-profit, not-for-profit, and public.

Spirituality has touched worship, education, counseling, and evangelism. It is now ready to touch administration. I believe that such a movement is afoot. I know that it is not mine, but God's. I am willing and excited to be a part of what God is doing.

PART 1

The Heart of the Matter: Transforming and Inspiring Church Boards

CHAPTER 1

Simple Elegance: The Spirit of a Board as "Worshipful Work"

Two Stories

First Presbyterian Church, Brandon, Florida

Conducting an interview with the session of First Church, I found an excited and energized group. They told me about their meeting agenda, fashioned after their Sunday morning worship order. (See appendix 1.) At the beginning of the meeting, they light a candle and sing a hymn; they occasionally share communion and seal their decisions with an offertory prayer.

One member said, "When I look at the agenda, I am constantly reminded that we are in worship here, even though we are doing the business of the church."

Another said, "We do less debating and arguing [than we used to]. We hear everybody's input. The worship agenda makes us think about a matter before we speak." They agreed that ever since the group had instituted a worship-centered agenda, the elders and committees had been coming to the meeting better prepared, with motions in hand. The meetings have been "uplifting," and they end on time. Members go home inspired and relaxed. Several recognized how different these meetings are from other boards on which they serve—Boy Scouts and county boards.

Their pastor, Paul Reiter, explained how this new agenda format came to be:

> A few years ago I came to recognize a mind set in the church at large which was built on organizational development principles.

(I as a pastor had been trained in them in the early seventies.) The old "board of directors" model with its management by objective and imposition of business principles dominated our church boards and meetings. I began to observe only a limited success with them and an increase in frustration. When pressed, the model broke down. One elder insisted that we do things the way they were done at Westinghouse, keeping the business of the church separate from anything spiritual.

During this same period of time, I took my annual week of reflection with the Trappists at their monastery in Conyers, Georgia. I observed their rhythms of the liturgy of the hours—all integrated into their work. I was invited to sit in on their meetings and saw how they integrated the spiritual life with business.

Out of these two experiences I began to explore an integrated format—first with small groups, church school classes, then with the coordinating council of the church. In 1991 we began to use a worship format in our session meetings, and we've been using it ever since. We have made some adjustments. Leadership of the worship elements is now shared by the laity. The clerk, for instance, lights the Christ candle to open the meeting. The chair of the worship committee selects and leads the hymns, etc.

Our "service" is built around the "Word," so we struggle to find the most appropriate setting for that. Our "offering" is the reports of committees. It is followed by offertory prayers, which have developed into very interactive participation, where the thanks and concerns of the church are lifted to God.

Would we go back to the old "business only" format? No way!

Trinity Lutheran Church, Shawnee Mission, Kansas

The pastor of Trinity Church (Missouri Synod) read an article I had written, "A New Look at Church Boards and Councils," published in the Kansas School of Religion paper. He connected with the themes immediately; he was looking for ways to further develop his church council. The church linked up with our Set Apart Lay Leaders project the following year.

Following the orientation retreat, I met regularly with the church's two pastors and the president of the council to map out plans for council meetings. Together we found ways to include story telling, reflection, and prayer in the meetings. The council president designated certain people to listen carefully for prayer "clues" during each meeting, then offer appropriate prayers before adjournment. The church was facing some personnel changes and a major renovation project. Careful planning, empowerment of all the council members, and grace notes of inspiration all helped the council and church to navigate successfully through some big decisions and point to new directions.

When one of the pastors suggested that the meeting agenda be designed like the church's popular Sunday morning contemporary service, steps were taken to implement the change—with some reservations expressed by the president. One motivating factor had been a guest preacher's sermon on "life and work as worship."

At the following planning meeting, the worship-structured agenda was written, complete with liturgical components and the necessary reports and decision items. When the meeting concluded, the president, a retired businessman with experience leading meetings in business circles and in the church, announced, "I just can't do it. Worship belongs in the sanctuary under the leadership of a pastor. This meeting is different." We struggled over this difficulty together, knowing that his reservations were a matter of deep conviction and personal integrity. After some discussion he suggested that the alternative worship agenda be passed out to the council members as a illustration of "worshipful work." But he insisted that he would have to moderate the meeting using an agenda with which he was more familiar and comfortable.

All of these discussions were open and respectful. Much integrity was exhibited by each person in the soul-searching struggle to plan and decide. Later in the week the pastor called me. He felt it would be best not to distribute the worship agenda, even though he saw its creative possibilities. It would put too much pressure on the president, who was also his friend. The pastor observed that the council president held the position of a pastor in such high esteem that the president felt presumptuous to assume a liturgical role as moderator of the meeting.

A Master Story: Genesis 22:1–17

After these things God tested Abraham. He said to him, "Abraham!" And he said, "Here I am." [God] said, "Take your son, your only son Isaac, whom you love, and go to the land of Moriah, and offer him there as a burnt offering on one of the mountains that I shall show you." So Abraham rose early in the morning, saddled his donkey, and took two of his young men with him, and his son Isaac; he cut the wood for the burnt offering, and set out and went to the place in the distance that God had shown him. On the third day Abraham looked up and saw the place far away. Then Abraham said to his young men, "Stay here with the donkey; the boy and I will go over there; we will worship, and then we will come back to you." Abraham took the wood of the burnt offering and laid it on his son Isaac, and he himself carried the fire and the knife. So the two of them walked on together. Isaac said to his father Abraham, "Father!" And he said, "Here I am, my son." He said, "The fire and the wood are here, but where is the lamb for a burnt offering?" Abraham said, "God himself will provide the lamb for a burnt offering, my son." So the two of them walked on together.

When they came to the place that God had shown him, Abraham built an altar there and laid the wood in order. He bound his son Isaac, and laid him on the altar, on top of the wood. Then Abraham reached out his hand and took the knife to kill his son. But the angel of the Lord called to him from heaven, and said, "Abraham, Abraham!" And he said, "Here I am." He said, "Do not lay your hand on the boy or do anything to him; for now I know that you fear God, since you have not withheld your son, your only son, from me." And Abraham looked up and saw a ram, caught in a thicket by its horns. Abraham went and took the ram and offered it up as a burnt offering instead of his son. So Abraham called that place "The Lord will provide"; as it is said to this day, "On the mount of the Lord it shall be provided."

The angel of the Lord called to Abraham a second time from heaven, and said, "By myself I have sworn, says the Lord: Because you have done this, and have not withheld your son, your only son, I will indeed bless you, and I will make your offspring as numerous as the stars of heaven and as the sand that is on the seashore."

Reflective Story Weaving

Few of us are called to put as much "on the line" as was Abraham, yet we are confronted and judged by his story. Like him, we are called to offer before God all that defines us and is important to us—yes, even our board work.

Places are important. The mountain was special to God and to Abraham. "Abraham called the place, 'The Lord will provide,' which led to a popular saying, "on the mountain of the Lord it shall be provided" (v. 14). Board tables, too, are (or ought to be) holy ground—places for sacrificial offerings and blessings.

People are hungry for inspiration—in worship, in vocations, in family life. The church looks for inspirational leadership, usually from pastors. But why not from the board as well? Could not the council be inspired or "in-spirited" and in turn provide inspiration for the whole church?

Webster defines *inspire* as (1) "to influence, move, or guide by divine or supernatural inspiration"; (2) "to exert an animating, enlivening, or exalting influence on." Isn't this what boards as well as individual people are seeking? And if a board is to be inbreathed by the Spirit of God, where better for it to happen than in worship?

At the first annual Set Apart Lay Leaders Collegium, the newly claimed culture of a board and its meetings was dubbed "worshipful work." In response, an advisory panel member spoke an inspired word: "The project cannot be complex and complicated or it will bog down. Instead, it must have at its core a 'simple elegance' which is inviting and illuminating." We believe the phrase *worshipful work* provides that simple elegance!

But since the model comes from the tradition of authentic faith communities and is biblically grounded, we must search for an image from scripture that can describe, inspire, and drive the model. Paul's letter to the church at Rome provides an image that can well be applied to boards.

Let's allow the structure of the text of Romans 12:1 to present the preferred culture of worshipful work.

I appeal
>   to you therefore, brothers and sisters,
>   by the mercies of God,
>   to present your bodies
>>   as a living
>>>   sacrifice,
>>   holy and acceptable
>>   to God,
>   which is your spiritual worship.

I Appeal . . .

The message is urgent. Much is at stake.

In fact, the very future of the church is at stake. Our congregations and denominations are in a state of reformulation, attempting to discover new patterns and forms that are at once faithful to their deep spiritual roots and appropriate for the twenty-first century.

The commitment of you who are board members is at stake. People will not go on serving unfulfilling, life-draining boards.

So in boardmanship the first step is to name the dis-ease or distress. Set Apart Lay Leaders project, in conjunction with Presbyterian Research Services, conducted a survey of 605 elders who were just coming off a three-year term of office. In response to an open-ended question about what surprised them, 155 registered positive responses, while 199 registered negative surprises. Twenty-nine percent reported that they were weary and burned out—a daunting figure when we consider its cumulative impact over a period of years, and a shameful statistic for an organization that desires new life and values every individual person.[1]

My son, a college sprinter, joined on to the track program of a major university. He soon noted that a lot of the sprinters were being injured in the training program. When he asked the coaches about it, they replied, "We fully expect that 20 percent of our sprinters will be injured. We are willing to accept that in order to get the others into the condition we want them in for competition." That may have been acceptable to the coaches, but not to my son. He transferred out at the semester break.

This kind of attrition is unacceptable both in college athletics and on church boards. Its consequences are devastating, both personally and corporately. The good news is that church boards can be revitalized.

And just as a burned-out board has tremendous power to affect a congregation negatively if it is severely conflicted, internally dysfunctional, or bogged down in a sticky mire of minutiae, so a revitalized board owns tremendous potential for good.

From a strategic standpoint, one who holds hope for the renewal of congregational life has to start somewhere. What better place to start than the board and its meetings! If those meetings and relationships are life giving rather than life draining, the board can become a model of community and ministry for the whole church. As I see it, the level of commitment in a congregation will not rise above that of the set apart leaders. The sense of community and care for one another will not rise above that of the consistory. The stewardship practices will not rise above those of the council. The prayer life will not rise above that of the board. The capacity to reflect biblically and theologically will not rise above that of the vestry. The willingness to take a prophetic position will not rise above that of the deacons. The hope and excitement for the future of the church will not rise above that of the session.

Too often a few church leaders who hold a vision for the church spend their energies working around the board. Why not apply those energies to the board? Such an investment can pay big dividends. The power to influence that emanates from a board is tremendous—for good or for ill. Revitalization is an urgent matter.

The urgency in this appeal is not limited to the internal life of the individual board member or to the board as a whole. The church must counter a set of dynamics in the entire social order that works against the creation of community.

. . . To You Therefore, Brothers and Sisters

For the previous eleven chapters of Romans, Paul has been wrestling with the dimensions and scope of God's grace. He has concluded that God's grace is sufficient for those both under and outside the law—for Jew and Gentile. A new people has been created, the likes of which the world has never seen. Reconciled by God through Jesus Christ, Jew and Gentile are now one family, equal in access to God's grace and gifts, equal in power to live out their calling in faithful ministries. There is no longer Jew or Greek, slave or free, male or female. All are one in Christ. Two thousand years later we have a hard time grasping how revolutionary Paul's thesis was!

The word *therefore* in Paul's writing is often a hinge on which an entire discourse turns. *Therefore* in Romans 12:1 follows Paul's exposition on reconciling grace, and it is placed directly in front of "brothers and sisters," indicating that community with one another before God is rooted in divine grace.

To apply Paul's word *you* to those who serve on boards and councils is simply to extend the principle. The council is not a second-class citizen or an advisory voice to the ears of power. Laypeople are empowered by virtue of their baptism, gifts, and calling by the Spirit. The voice of the congregation has set them apart by installation (or in some cases ordination) to do a work of ministry called leadership. They are not representatives of special groups or interests in the church. They are set apart to seek God's will for the church and its ministry in the world. What's more, the ethos or character of the congregation is manifest in the composition of the council, lending it great authority to get things done. What empowerment!

Self-perception is crucial. The individual board member is not to see her- or himself as merely a program manager serving the pastoral CEO or as a political representative of other interests, but as a *spiritual leader* with gifts and power to act.

The collective board is not to see itself as a coordinating cabinet or an advisory group but as the people of God in community. The group is the body of Christ, with members having varying gifts, wisdom, and functions. As such the group's life is formed by scripture, prayer, silent waiting, witnessing, and serving. Members are on a journey together that may take them on paths to the wilderness, into the arenas of ambiguity and conflict, or to pleasant meadows of discovery, satisfaction, and delight.

The meeting will no longer be seen as a gathering of individual people with business to transact, but as the functioning of the body with all its patterns, disciplines, and ministries.

The goal of the board will not be to advance individual agendas or stroke personal egos, but to hold in trust the life of the community and its ministry. When an owner of land, property, business, or financial assets really "gets" the psalmist's vision that "the earth is the Lord's and the fulness thereof" (Ps. 24:1 KJV), everything is put in a new perspective —of stewardship. The same can be said of trust-holding by boards as stewards of the community of faith, the church, and its life and ministry.

Imagine a banner hung over a board table: "A Community of

Spiritual Leaders." Think of the difference it would make if everyone believed those words and acted with that self-awareness!

One visitor to a number of board meetings where a worship-structured model is being tested observed,

> There is a definite sense of call to ministry and a definite sense of community among the board members. People think about and get excited about the ministry of the board. Board members have a sense of working toward God's agenda and God's glory instead of their own.

. . . By the Mercies of God

One side of the "therefore" hinge holds a new community of brothers and sisters. The other side of the hinge is securely fastened to "the mercies of God." Therefore because of the mercies of God we are a community and are urged toward a particular course of action.

In the previous eleven chapters, Paul has been laying out God's plan of salvation for Jew and Gentile. He concludes that God is merciful to all, even though none deserve it. When the limitations of words and concepts fail to plumb the depths of God's mercy, Paul breaks into a hymn of praise for the mystery and wonder of it all. "O the depth of the riches and wisdom and knowledge of God! . . . For from him and through him and to him are all things. To him be the glory forever. Amen" (11:33, 36).

Here, Paul offers a pole star whereby we get our bearings—a fixed point of reference. If all things are from God, if all things are routed through God, if all things flow to God, then our only appropriate response is one of praise, worship, and service. We are to live our individual and collective lives "solely to the glory of God."

Sole gloria was John Calvin's theme and motto. That heavenly orientation did not remove Calvin from the hard tasks of the world. It took him and his board of elders into the affairs of the people in the streets and into the chambers of the town council. Nothing was outside the purview of God's grace, judgment, and loving reign.

The "mercies of God" invite boards and councils into gracious space. No one deserves to be there. No one is smart enough or powerful enough or loving enough or caring enough. God has called out a people, including leaders with special graces, to accomplish his mission. The "therefore" lives on!

An old story relates an angel's conversation with Jesus just after Jesus gave the Great Commission and ascended into heaven. The angel said, "Jesus, you have given them plan A. But what is plan B?"

"There is no plan B," Jesus replied. "I have entrusted them with the mission."

The heavenly mandate to live and act to God's glory is directed to church boards and councils. But the mandate does not come "unfunded." It is accompanied by "mercies"—many of them tender and some of them firm. God's Spirit, according to Paul in Romans 8, prays for, feeds, supports, and guides along the way.

Our response begins and ends in praise. In between we are to seek and live for the glory of God, and to transform all we are and all we do into an offering. That is where the culture of "worshipful work" for boards enters the picture.

. . . To Present

The image of the sacrificial altar dominates the Old Testament. The offering was to be prepared and then released to God. Releasing—taking one's hand off, letting go, surrendering—is so necessary but so difficult. It was difficult for Abraham when instructed to give up the only son of the promise. It must have been difficult for those who presented to God the firstborn from their flocks and herds.

One of the vital elements in spiritual formation is the willingness to relinquish all to God. We fear that complete surrender to God of the will either renders one a "nobody" or leaves one completely lost and obliterated in the vastness of God.

Thomas Merton invites the pilgrim to shed the "false self" in relinquishment—to discover one's true self in God. The paradox is that we gain by losing; we find when we surrender.

The New Testament also calls for relinquishment. If Jesus had not "emptied himself" by taking the basin and towel and washing feet, we would not have that powerful image of servant leadership before us. If there were no baptism, no casting off of old garments, no dying with Christ in the water, there could be no new garments, no rising with Christ into new life.

We tend to see spirituality in individual terms—I, me, and my. But spirituality is also corporate. The board as a community is also called to let go—to relinquish its own idea of what it ought to be. Bonhoeffer calls this self-designed vision of the community a "wish dream" and warns that it must be destroyed before real community can happen.[2] Community is not created or manufactured or designed; it happens only through God's grace. Community comes as pure gift.

If this is so, then all other board cultures that creep into the board room promising "effective boards" need to be relinquished.

How does this happen? Several boards with which we work begin their meetings with communion. In one meeting the presiding host asked, "What do these elements mean to us: the bread broken and the wine poured out?" The members' responses were not only an occasion for centering, but also a way of stripping away the self-will that sticks all over an agenda. Bible studies on the images of broken bread and poured wine can lead into reflection about what the board is holding on to or needs to let go of. Prayers of confession, both corporate and individual, both spoken and silent, can deepen the process.

Silence can also facilitate relinquishment. In it we are freed from the temptation to overpower one another with words and ideas. A board can focus and move much more effectively after it has experienced a conscious and corporate stripping away.

An elderly Trappist monk was being interviewed for a documentary on his community. When asked what his purpose in life was, he replied, "I am preparing my life as a beautiful gift which I will one day offer to God in my death."

Death is the ultimate "letting go." Each day the monk seemed to be practicing the art of shedding the false self and discovering his true self.

For boards, as for Trappist monks, the shedding is an offering.

. . . Your Bodies

The Greek word Paul chooses is not *sarx*, meaning "of the flesh" (muscle, bone, fluids), but *soma*—"all that defines who we are."

When we introduce ourselves, we normally define ourselves through a set of particular relationships (place, time, relationships, vocation, personality type, feelings, possessions, stories, dreams, values). *Soma* names the encompassing category through which we say to the world, "I am somebody."

Every board has its own *soma*, which has historic, relational, and value aspects. For boards and councils, defining categories include composition, organization, communication, activities, behaviors, customs, decision–making processes, management of ministry, agendas, goals, stories of failure and success, desires, and reputations. A printed agenda and the minutes of a meeting—along with the official documents of church governance and an organizational chart—will provide a few clues to the board's *soma*. For the church in Brandon, Florida, the agenda lists the reports of the committees as "the offering." The prayer that followed was really an offertory prayer.

Paul uses the plural form of *soma*—bodies, meaning there is a collection of what individual people bring. But the focus soon shifts to the corporate, for in the same chapter Paul speaks of one body with many parts—eyes, hands, hidden parts, and so forth.

A board's soma has a peculiar shape, based on the composition of the board by the individual members and the way they relate with one another. The group is a tender community always in formation as pastors and lay leaders come and go. People pass through the entrance and exit doors at the same time of the year. How they are led to say "hello" and "good-bye" will lend a flavor to the board as community. Assimilation of new board members requires time to hear their stories and recognize their gifts. Trinity Church takes time in retreats and at the opening portion of each meeting to listen to each council member and build a community life.

Release of exiting members involves several offerings: a naming and feeling of the grief, expressions of affirmation and thanks, and mutual exploration of arenas for ongoing lay ministry.

. . . As a Living Sacrifice

Just as the altar, the place of offering, is sacred and set apart, so the board room is holy ground. The board table is no less important than the commu-nion table. Both are receptacles and distribution centers for sacred gifts.

When the gathering around a board table is intentionally prayerful and worshipful, it seems natural for all the aspects of a worship service, including the offering, to find their way in. But instead of passing the plate for money, the "stuff" of the meeting is lifted, released, and dedicated to God.

Note that the Romans 12 bodies (plural) are now one offering (singular). Paul will not allow us to get too entrenched in individualism.

In the Hebrew tradition the sacrifice was always a corporate act. At one stage, the people offered the sacrifice and the priest ate as a symbol of unity. At another point, the people offered the sacrifice and then shared it as a fellowship meal.

"The trouble with living sacrifices," observed a leader in the Salvation Army, "is that they always want to crawl down off of the altar!" Offering and relinquishment are often scary and fraught with peril. Paul may even have had martyrdom in mind. No matter what the opposition or difficulty, he may be suggesting, offer yourselves even to the point of death. A few people who refuse to sell out at any price may have the courage of martyrdom. Some sects may even make a corporate pact of death, as do some who are bonded in devotion to a great cause such as the civil rights struggle. But boards? You decide.

Some people have warned that any effort to integrate spirituality and administration will make things more difficult rather than easier for boards. Conflicts and differences may deepen. Led by some deep, emerging biblical convictions, a board may choose to follow a prophetic course that may not be palatable to the congregation or to the larger church. That is a risk that must be faced. We must have confidence that actions grounded in discipleship and stewardship will yield a harvest of faithfulness. You don't have to be a gambler to hunger for some authentic risk taking.

. . . Holy and Acceptable to God

The living sacrifice, the offering up of the stuff of boards, is now visible from two perspectives—God's and ours.

From God's vantage point this offering is holy and acceptable. It may seem a poor substitute for the elaborate sacrificial system of Old Testament times, but even then God through the prophets had already announced that God despised feasts and sacrifices unless they were accompanied by justice and righteousness in relation to neighbor and the human community. God enters into a real world via the Spirit and works for reconciliation, justice, and peace at all levels. God is more interested in the transformation of life than in ritualizing dead symbols. Board work that is toward that end is an acceptable offering.

Might this be God's way—to live by dying? To be strong in weakness? To be wise in simplicity? To have by letting go? To lead by serving? Is this the nature of a spiritual world that society does not understand? Councils and boards might play a different tune and march to a different drummer. The primary "public" to be served by a board could be God alone—much like the football player answering a question about the difficulty of playing before sixty–five thousand booing and cheering people: "I only play for one person. That's the coach. I play his way!"

. . . Which Is Your Spiritual Worship

Let us offer a new perspective for the board's offering—that of "spiritual worship." The preferred culture of a board now has a name and an accompanying image or picture. The term, spiritual worship, invites us to say, "This is our kind of meeting. This is our kind of community. This is our kind of calling."

Discerning

The discerning eye that searches for the mind and will of God can spot board cultures that are life enhancing and inspiring—full of the Spirit of God. The eye can also sort out cultures that are boring, lifeless, marching to the beat of a different spirit.

A look at the agenda of boards that are intentional about integrating spirituality and administration can reveal a "worship culture" that looks something like a Sunday morning worship order. A board like that of First Church, Brandon, stands in stark contrast to "culture X" boards, which borrow their formats from outside the church. Here are some typical elements in worship-oriented agenda.

Gathering in God's Name

The gathering call is centered in the presence, will, and purpose of God. God existed before there ever was a board or a church. Attributes of God are identified and praised. God's presence is invoked. God is recognized as the meeting host whose agenda is being considered. A hymn may be sung that focuses upon who God is and what the church is to be about.

In contrast, a culture-X church board gathers in response to a set of by-laws or the call for a meeting. Its purpose is fixed by agreed-upon goals. A collection of minds and egos gathers out of the strengths the group brings from education and experience.

Story Telling

Personal faith journeys are told or touched upon. Members identify and reflect upon experiences of the church in which God is recognized as an active player. The group considers a "master story" from the biblical tradition. They offer prayers of thanksgiving or confession that grow out of the stories. A particular issue before the board prompts the study of a relevant scripture.

The culture-X church board receives reports and plans. Members may tell personal stories, but some will avoid being personal, preferring to stick with the business at hand.

Responding to God's Word

In ordering the life and ministry of the church, a worship-oriented board attempts to agree on what to pray for. It may be something far beyond reach. But part of the work is to form the prayer, remembering Matthew 18:19: "If two of you agree on earth about anything you ask, it will be done for you." Recognizing that they "have not because they ask not," the council works at a focus for prayer.

This group holds before God the needs in the church and the world that are beyond their capacity to meet. Intercession is a work to be done.

They make decisions, attempting to discern God's will and call in various settings.

They may insert belief statements or make a corporate statement of belief about God through one of the historic creeds of the church.

In contrast, church board X seeks to do what it thinks best in light of the organization's purpose. They do what they can with what they have.

Going in Peace

The worship-oriented board may conclude with reflections on the meeting, where members name differences or unfinished work. Some pastoral "mending" and caring may need to be done. An attempt is made to wrap up the meeting in such a way that a second "after-meeting in the parking lot" is not necessary.

An elder from the Brandon church observed, "I am able to go home from the meeting and go right to sleep. I used to have to debrief for an hour with my wife and unwind before going to bed."

In contrast, board X members may go home restless. Business-as-usual boards we have interviewed report a much higher incidence of conflict, frustration, and gossip.

Summary of Culture of Spirituality

The offering of our work surely does make sense. Church boards are faith communities. As such it follows that the culture of their life should incorporate the culture of the church.

The word spirituality still tends to hang people up. It is not part of the jargon of board meetings. Some see it as a white, puffy cloud floating by that has nothing to do with reality.

But the word spirituality is too good to give up, for we do govern from a base of the spirit. We must continually seek to fathom its full meaning, which will compel board members to grapple with hard issues and callings.

The dividends are great. A church board working in the Spirit is delightful to watch. One board impressed an observer as a group completely devoted to its faith and to its church:

> This is a group of people who are trying to make a difference in the community in which the church serves. They are full of enthusiasm, pride, and a strong sense of being called to minister through that particular body.

This picture of spirituality continues in the observer's notes:

> In the churches in which the project seems to be working, there is a

definite sense of call to ministry, and a definite sense of community among the board members. They know and share the goals of the project. Despite the topic of the meeting, the troubles or blessings of the church, the meetings were fulfilling spiritually, personally, and socially. These board members seemed to have a sense of truly serving God and the community . . . working for God's agenda and God's glory instead of their own.

And the tension also continues. The observer noted:

In the churches where there were members who were not on board (no pun intended) with the project's goals, members were unwilling to change. The spiritual reflection and story telling aspects of the agenda were treated as unnecessary and a waste of time. These meetings were cold and businesslike. It seemed like people were there to show what they could do, not see what God can do.

Our observers began to look for an encouraging indicator: the ease of movement back and forth between prayer and business or between scripture reflection and discussion. Our emphasis has been on integration within the agenda, not on establishing disjointed segments. This ease of movement is a sign that integration is possible.

The Vision

The participants in the Set Apart Lay Leaders project offer a vision of a culture of worshipful work or prayerful gathering. Some would call it a unique paradigm that changes the whole perspective of board work. "So if anyone is in Christ, there is a new creation; everything old has passed away; see, everything has become new!" (2 Cor. 5:17).

Chrysler Corporation introduced a new car model with the advertising slogan "This changes everything!" When Galileo offered a new view of the solar system, it did in fact change everything. One true picture changed a whole set of distorted perspectives. Nothing was the same anymore.

Perhaps this new vision of board work is in reality something ancient—a distinct archetype. Webster describes an archetype as "an original pattern of knowledge, belief, behavior, and forms."

Once people "get it"—discover the paradigm (discussed fully in chapters 3 through 6), recognize the archetype—everything does in fact change! A board will no longer be "business as usual." A whole new organizing principle is unleashed.

Implementation: Ways to Pray in Board Meetings

Members of a church council used the term *book–end prayers* to refer to the perfunctory way in which prayer can be scheduled and offered at the beginning and close of the meeting. It traditionally separates out the spiritual aspects of the meeting from the "business at hand." The business part of the meeting still resembles the process that one would typically see in extrachurch circles—an emphasis on efficiency, a reliance on "reasoned" judgments, and a structure by parliamentary rules, all ordered by a litany of reports with recommendations and decisions voted by majority rule.

If we redefine the activity of the people of God serving on church boards and see it as worshipful work, then prayer no longer can be relegated to a book-end position; it will saturate the agenda and thread its way throughout the meeting.

Church boards that are "doing board differently" are discovering ways to allow prayer to permeate the whole meeting. Here are several ways:

Frame Prayers to Agenda

Frame traditional opening and closing prayers in relation to the agenda of the meeting. The invocation might focus on the image of God and create an openness to and awareness of the Spirit's presence and leading. The closing prayer might be a thankful offertory for the work of the meeting––lifted to God. Preparing for a night's restful sleep invites prayers of release and relinquishment, an acknowledgment that boards cannot maintain control. Entrust the stuff of a meeting to God in the same way you prepare for sleep—by "letting go."

Intersperse Prayers of Thanksgiving

Follow each committee report or grouping of stories with prayers of
thanksgiving. Imagine that the "stuff" of the stories is piled on the table
before you. Sort through the stuff and identify occasions for thanksgiving. Ask a designated member to voice a prayer. Or the whole group
could participate in naming each blessing and responding in unison ("We
give you thanks, O Lord") or by singing a responsive line from a familiar
hymn or song with a thanksgiving theme, such as "Now Thank We All
Our God."

Glean for Prayer

Glean the meeting for prayer and praise. From my boyhood days on the
farm I remember that Gleaner was a brand name for a combine, a ma-
chine that separated the seed from the chaff and straw. At the beginning
of a meeting, you might assign four people to keep notes with an eye
toward separating out items for prayer. (They do not record the decisions being made. That is the task of the recording secretary.) One
should note anything that would be the basis for thanksgiving. Another
would record needs or opportunities in the church or wider world that
call for intercession. Still another would note situations within the board
itself that would be the basis for prayers of petition. The fourth would
note the work of the Spirit of God in the life of the council or congregation. At the end of the meeting, focus worship on the four areas of
thanksgiving, intercession, petition, and praise.

Offer Prayers of Confession

Offer prayers of confession. One worship order I have seen includes the
sentence "We admit how we are." Confession covers not only errors and
sins, but also weariness, frustration, confusion, elation, boredom, fulfillment, and so forth. Perhaps this broader definition lies behind the agenda of the meeting of First Church in Brandon. Pastor Reiter's report was
followed by "prayers of confession"! He is not one who lays a heavy
guilt trip on the board; he is insightful and honest. The prophets in the
scriptural tradition were "seers," those who had sight for things as they

actually were. Naming "how things really are" and "what is left undone" are healthy processes for a board. But by themselves they can bind and paralyze a board; the board needs to have "some place to take it." Try "amazing grace"!

If both the congregation and board have a corporate life, the board's confession can also be corporate. In an era of individualism in our culture and faith, understanding corporate spirituality is difficult. Perhaps confession is a good starting place.

Sing Prayers

Sing the prayers. Send each board member home with the church hymn book and the assignment to select one verse of any hymn that best captures the most appropriate prayer for the church at the present time. Sing these hymns throughout the meeting. Many boards have never sung together and discover unusual talent! The blending of many voices also moves the council along the path of corporate spirituality. Often discussion and discourse are anything but harmonious. Singing together models the harmony to which they aspire. The presence of wonder and mystery in music also helps break up the rational framework of most meetings by adding some "grace notes."

"Time Out" for Prayer

Take "time out" for prayer. After twenty minutes of debate and discussion over an issue on which people seem divided, the egos take over. Some deliberative groups have found value in taking three to five minutes of silent "time out" for personal refocusing and prayer. Let each one silently consider these questions: *Am I closing myself off from information that we need to make this decision? Whom do I need to forgive to be more fully present here? What is an image of God that needs to come to bear in this setting? How does the scripture that we read shed light on us now? Am I operating in a need-to-win or need-to-save-face mode? How would servant leaders make this decision?* Time out periods could be called by a strict clock setting by the meeting moderator or by any member who requests it at any time for any reason.

Rotate Prayer

At the beginning of the meeting assign each person to a certain fifteen-minute segment of the meeting; during that assigned time, members should pray silently for each person in the group and for the deliberative process in which the board is engaged. Tilden Edwards, director of the Shalem Institute in Washington, D.C., attests to the dramatic difference this rotating prayer can make in the tone of the gathering as all are being held before God in a loving and caring manner.[3]

Draw upon Model Prayers of Scripture

When educational consultant Donald Griggs was asked in a recent workshop how one might begin to use the Bible in committee meetings, he advised, "Don't introduce it as a new, complicated program. Just start doing it because that is what the people of God do. It won't be long until they can't remember doing it any other way!" The following samples are suggestive—certainly not exhaustive!

The Psalms can be used so many ways. You might try this: Have someone read a psalm slowly and deliberately. Invite any who would like to ponder a phrase say "yes" out loud. The reader will stop for one to three minutes of silence, then continue reading until the next "yes."

The Lord's Prayer contains many phrases that rhythmically rise and fall. These phrases can be attached to the inhaling and exhaling of one's breath and could be experienced together as a common centering discipline.

Jesus' prayer for his friends and disciples (John 17) contains a cluster of specific petitions beginning with "that they may . . ." Let the board choose the petition that is most appropriate in the board's current situation.

Paul's heartfelt prayer of thanksgiving for his friends (Phil. 1:3–11) can be used in a special way when new board members are coming on or when others are exiting. Identify aspects of the "heart life" of which Paul speaks that the board can value for its own life. See where that applies to transitions within the board.

Claim Paul's great prayer for the church (Eph. 3:14-21) for your board. Find ways to report back how that prayer is being lived out during and between meetings!

In Matthew 18:19-20 Jesus invited his followers to "agree on" what to pray for. One of the boards with which we worked reported, only partly in jest, that they were still trying to come to agreement on what their prayer would be! The most significant decision a board can make is about what its prayer will be. The prayer is not a strategic plan to be accomplished but a petition that cannot be accomplished by our own efforts.

Acknowledge Subliminal Prayer

Prayer may be ceaseless and subliminal, even when we engage in active work or deliberation. Such prayer plays just below the conscious level. The old desert saints wanted to pray without ceasing, so they attached the Jesus Prayer ("Lord Jesus Christ, have mercy upon me, a sinner") to the rising and falling of their breath. For a while the breath carries the prayer. Then in a mystical moment the prayer carries the breath without one's thinking about it!

I have often had a hymn come to mind for no apparent reason and stay with me for hours or days. Though it may come and go in my consciousness, it seems to play on as subliminal prayer whether I am mentally aware of it or not.

For boards, subliminal prayer may be stimulated by symbols that remind members of God's love and presence. One board lights a lamp at the beginning of every meeting as a way of claiming Christ's light and presence at the table. The lamp is extinguished at the close of the meeting; members are exhorted to carry the light on in their individual and collective lives.

One session has homemade stoles personalized for each elder and presented at their ordination or installation service. The stole represents the yoke and the yoking of each elder to Christ. The stole is worn by the elder at every official church function in which the elder has a leadership role. And it is worn by all elders while sitting in session.

Follow a Sunday Worship Order

To remind themselves that they are doing worshipful work, some councils have constructed their agenda within the same worship framework used in Sunday morning worship. Members connect with the obvious reminders that they are in session to do the Lord's work.

Use Ordered Liturgies and Litanies

Too often these are used in the early part of a meeting and then laid aside. But they lend themselves very well for use at transitions and intervals throughout the meeting. The brief and simple worship orders of the Taize Community in France, for example, can be portioned out over the course of the assembly. The common prayers add to the richness of a varied prayer menu.

Conclusion

We sometimes fear that our efforts to establish dynamic themes in board development will be reduced to a set of mechanical procedures. But the rich sources of imagination, tradition, and daily practices mitigate against a hardening of the spiritual arteries.

The observers-evaluators who visited the meetings of the churches with which we worked commented on the worshipful expressions they saw. One observer noted:

> Each meeting incorporated some sort of worship time into the agenda, including the reading of scripture, prayer, the singing of hymns, and even communion. By far the most moving was the sharing of communion by the members who passed the elements to one another while the group sang a hymn. Following communion, the members shared prayer requests with each other. What I had thought was a rather formal meeting turned into a very tender and sweet fellowship of God's people.

Music is rarely used in council meetings. But many of our boards are setting a hymn book on the table alongside the Bible and agenda. One pastor who had just returned from a sabbatical led the group in singing "Angels Watching over Me." That led to a discussion of ways in which both pastor and council had been "watched over." Their discussion was framed by music and scripture. Another board sang three hymns—opening, middle, and closing. Yet another laced the meeting with three verses of "We Gather Together to Ask the Lord's Blessing."

We see the fellowship meal and communion creeping into more and more board meetings, a link to the tradition of the early church, where the table was a frequent forum for decision making.

Resistance to framing the work of a board as worship tends to come from the conviction that "there is a place for everything and everything should be in its place." Worship belongs to Sunday and sanctuary. Bible study belongs to Sunday school. Prayer belongs to worship.

But an inspirational "moment" in a meeting does wonders in loosening the strings of resistance! And those inspirational moments will come once worshipful work is attempted. Let the only rule be "meetings are worship." All else will flow to and from that fountain. Then we can drink from its fullness!

CHAPTER 2

Creeping Cultures: The Spirits of the Agenda of Board Meetings

A Story:
First Presbyterian Church, Bartlesville, Oklahoma

Several years ago the pastor and several key elders from First Church in Bartlesville came to a conference called *The Elder as Spiritual Leader*. There they noted that the corporate ways of the city's leading employer, Phillips Petroleum, were being mimicked in the boards of organizations all over town, including the churches. They wondered if there was a different way—one more attune with the ethos of the church. They picked up a few clues in the conference and went home to work on it. Recently I visited that church and sat in on one of their board meetings.

Fourteen board members and four staff were gathered around the table. The meeting lasted two hours and followed an agenda prepared by the pastor and clerk.

The meeting was lively, with active and spirited participation. Seventy-eight verbal contributions were made in addition to those of the moderator. While recording statements within various categories, I was surprised that occasions for humor ranked number one. These people were actually having fun in a board meeting! They knew when to break the tension and when to add energy to the meeting with their humor!

As the meeting drew to a close, they asked me if I would mind sharing observations of what I had seen and heard.

I reported, "What you did most and best was laugh. You shared fifty-two good, hearty, corporate laughs." With that they laughed again, and one said, "Fifty-three." And so it went up to sixty before another person pleaded, "Okay. We get the point. Knock it off!"

I continued, "You made thirteen statements of belief, meaning, or value. Eight different times you referred to biblical images, themes, or stories that led you to those reflections.

"Twelve times you directed specific tending gestures to other members of the board with expressions of thanks, appreciation, and affirmation. These were tender moments.

"You reported deliberations of other groups seven times, shared information that you needed ten times, asked eight questions, and shared eight stories of specific events.

"One of your corporate stories took twenty minutes to tell—the one in which you used 'and then' or 'but before that' as lead lines to each of your contributions. You discovered that no one had the whole story, but each of you had an important part of it. The story is now owned and enriched by your group participation.

"Yet in the course of this meeting you made only four decisions, most of these without 'pro' and 'con' debate but only with clarification of information until you discovered that your decision was already made.

"You sang two hymns together and prayed six times. Some of your prayers were shared as part of a unison liturgy. Others were voiced in relation to particular people (a new member, a departing staff member) or needs."

After the meeting the clerk and I fell into a conversation about recording the official meeting minutes. If the sole purpose of the meeting was to transact business, then the four actions was the whole story. But there was so much more. It was a prayerful gathering, a joyous celebration of stories, people, ministries, and the good news of the gospel. It was inspirational. Not only were members moved to laughter, but they were moved to tears. Time "stood still" on a number of occasions as people simply savored the moment. How could all of this be captured in the record of the meeting? It is etched in the memory of the people who experienced those special moments.

A Master Story:
Minutes of Four Council Meetings, Jerusalem

Minutes of Meeting 1: Based on Acts 1:12–26

The meeting was held in a large upstairs room, where the eleven disciples were gathered with Mary and her sons, women who were followers, and others. Total attendance: 120. Peter was concerned that a twelfth disciple be chosen to replace Judas, who had come to a disastrous end. He quoted David, suggesting that another was to take Judas's place. To qualify, the nominees must have been followers from the beginning and witnesses to the Resurrection.

The assembled body nominated two candidates: Matthias and Joseph.

> Then they prayed and said, "Lord, you know everyone's heart. Show us which one of these two you have chosen. . . . " And they cast lots for them, and the lot fell on Matthias; and he was added to the eleven apostles (vv. 24, 26).

Minutes of Meeting 2: Based on Acts 6:1–6

A complaint had been registered by the Greek-speaking Christians that their widows were being neglected in the food distribution. So the twelve called a meeting of the total community to consider the matter.

The twelve were so busy praying and teaching the Word of God to this growing church that they didn't have time to serve tables. They suggested that seven people be selected with the qualifications of being trustworthy, wise, and full of the Spirit. The community was pleased to choose seven Greek speakers. "They had these men stand before the apostles, who prayed and laid their hands on them" (v. 6).

Minutes of Meeting 3: Based on Acts 11:1–18

The meeting was called by the apostles and other believers, having heard that Peter was coming to town. Some were upset that he was associating with Gentiles and wanted to know why.

Peter told his story in great detail—his dream, his meeting with the Gentile Cornelius in his home, and how the Holy Spirit fell on Cornelius' household while Peter was preaching.

> "I remembered the word of the Lord, how he had said, 'John baptized with water, but you will be baptized with the Holy Spirit.' If then God gave them the same gift that he gave us when we believed in the Lord Jesus Christ, who was I that I could hinder God?" When [the council] heard this, they were silenced. And they praised God, saying, "Then God has given even to the Gentiles the repentance that leads to life" (vv. 16–18).

Minutes of Meeting 4: Based on Acts 15:1–35

The meeting of the apostles and elders in Jerusalem was called at the request of the church in Antioch. Conflict had arisen when several from the Jerusalem church who were teaching in Antioch insisted that Gentile Christians should observe the ritual laws of Moses—particularly the rite of circumcision.

Paul and Barnabas, who disagreed with these Jerusalem teachers, were sent to Jerusalem by the Antioch church to discuss the issue. They were warmly welcomed by the Jerusalem church, which was eager to hear their stories of the conversion of the Gentiles.

The issue at hand was addressed, there being intense debate on both sides. Peter, in particular, spoke eloquently about the gift of the Spirit to the Gentiles and of salvation by the grace of the Lord Jesus Christ alone.

When Paul and Barnabas spoke, there was a silent hush. Their stories of signs and wonders swayed the assembly. Then James, the brother of the Lord Jesus, spoke the mind of the whole group. He cited Simeon's prediction that Gentiles would believe, then said the church should lay off troubling the believers at Antioch. The assembly consented, then chose two of their own members, Judas called Barsabbas and Silas, to carry a letter back to the church at Antioch. The letter read,

> . . . We have decided unanimously to choose representatives and send them to you. . . . It has seemed good to the Holy Spirit and to us to impose on you no further burden than these essentials; that you abstain from what has been sacrificed to idols and from blood and

from what is strangled and from fornication. If you keep yourselves
from these, you will do well. Farewell" (vv. 25, 28–29).

Reflective Story Weaving

In weaving the stories together, certain common threads appear:
- The membership of the meetings is inclusive—men, women, apostles, elders, Greek-speaking Christians, and people with varying
  opinions. All bore varying degrees of wisdom.
- They met in a context of respect and warm hospitality. Joy was
  expressed even in the midst of potentially damaging conflict.
- The agenda were simple, straightforward, and easy to understand—
  issues being vacancy, neglect, inclusion, and ritual.
- Specific stories were told—the plight of Judas, neglect of the widows, the conversion of Cornelius, a dispute in Antioch.
- The biblical tradition was drawn upon as a basis for discussion and
  decision making. David, Jesus, Simeon, and the scriptures were
  cited.
- Beliefs and values rose from this touch with tradition. This is seen
  in the standards for the selection of leaders, in the affirmation that
  the Spirit is the same gift to all, and in the doctrine that salvation is
  by grace rather than ritual order. These values formed a foundation
  for decisions.
- Discernment of God's leading is sought in the deep places of the
  heart, in silence, and in discussion and debate. The whole community, including apostles and elders, possessed wisdom born of the
  presence of the Spirit. ("Show us which one . . . you have chosen"
  [Acts 1]). At the same time, they avoided taking themselves too
  seriously, exhibiting a kind of "holy flippancy" by casting lots for
  God's choice!
- Their decisions were initiated by people with the gift of special
  wisdom but always confirmed by the body in consensus.
- Prayer, worship, and praise framed and laced their meetings.
- They took specific steps to implement their decisions. Matthias was
  "added" to the twelve—engrafted as he entered. The group laid
  hands on "the seven" and offered prayers as they were sent forth.
  A letter was written, carried, and read to a church in need.

Discerning

On the heels of Paul's invitation to offer all in worship (Rom. 12:1) comes a teaching on transformation. Romans 12:2 provides structure through which we can apply the teaching on transformation to church boards.

> Do not be conformed to this world,
> > but be transformed by the renewal of your minds,
> > > so that you may discern
> > > > what is the will of God
> > > —what is good
> > > > and acceptable
> > > > and perfect.

Do Not Be Conformed to This World

From this phrase we might see two pictures of board or council conformity. One view is offered by J. B. Phillips, who paraphrases this: "Don't let the world around you squeeze you into its own mold." Board patterns that are "out there" in the world may assume a "gospel truth" posture and attempt to dominate the church council.

First Church of Bartlesville was located in a "company town," in which the local economy was tied to the success of that one industry. The company maintained a corporate image and behavior that permeated the whole city—government, not-for-profit organizations, even church boards. The session of First Church sought to find its own way as a distinct faith community, but its ways and means were continually compared and contrasted to the corporate ways of the company.

The second picture of "be not conformed" is more true to the meaning of the text and can be phrased this way: "Don't let the world break you apart or shatter you." There is not just one board culture out there but many disparate voices that can in effect drive a rudderless ship in most any direction, depending on the prevailing winds of the day.

The Gerasene demoniac whom Jesus encountered fits this picture (Luke 8). He said his name was Legion, indicating that he had many names. And he was out of control. He had to be bound for his own safety. It is possible for boards to have many names and feel many influences from the creeping cultures. An individual member of the board may import cultural strands that fit the member's comfort level, enable the member to exhibit special wisdom, or simply help get the member's ego stroked. The cumulative effect is hurtful to the individual members and to the life of the council as a whole.

After serving for fifteen years on a college board of trustees, I recognized that everyone had a speech to make—lawyers, bankers, preachers, business executives, school administrators, farmers, counselors, and so forth—and that all received self-affirmation and recognition through their speeches. I could almost predict what speech would be made in relation to a given subject. (And yes, I recognized what mine was.) Some would see that speech making as an important part of the decision-making process, for it brought many sides of wisdom to an issue. But I observed that it was a murky and inadequate way of community formation, often blurring our focus and preventing us from getting to the depths of the matter.

Our age can be quite precise in naming the systems, forces, and behaviors that hold sway over life. A consumption-production society, a market-driven economy, or a violence-prone drug and gun culture may all work against the creation of community. At the same time, we're quite adept at using names to blur reality. Greed raises its ugly head in many of our institutions and movements, but it will likely come disguised as "capital gains exclusions" or "fiscal responsibility."

Naming the demons and claiming the name of Christ is a way to curtail their power over us. Could angels be demons we are able to name?

To be unwittingly controlled by the nameless demons of "this world" is antithetical to the gospel. When we have named our demons, we are free to center on Christ as our unifying focus; we can then appropriate what we need from the world to move forward in his mission. Consider the following names of board room demons. Each discussion starts with a self-evaluating litmus question to be asked of a board. (See appendix 2, "Board Culture Indicators," for a questionnaire your board might use for self-evaluation and reflection.)

Advisory culture. A litmus question: *What special wisdom do you have that the people responsible for the program of the church rely upon?* (Is there also an expectation that your dollars will accompany the wisdom?)

Advisory boards wield the rubber stamp. Certain kinds of churches tend to develop advisory-type boards: church traditions where the pastor has been the sole authority figure; new and fast-growing churches built around the charisma and leadership of a strong pastor; or churches led by pastors with high control needs and authoritarian operating styles.

The effect of Vatican II on the governance process of the Roman Catholic Church presents an interesting case study. Twenty-five years after Vatican II commended councils at all levels of church life, only 66 to 75 percent of U.S. parishes have such councils, carried out in a wide variety of styles. Given the role the priest traditionally held in running a parish, it was natural that the first round of councils were advisory. As diocesan leadership worked with parish councils, they were permitted to assume more and more responsibility. Since the priest still has final authority, a strong determining factor in how the council develops is how the priest relates to it and blesses its life and work. Consensus decision making and use of a discernment process (in the selection of the council and in its method of coming to decisions) are smoothing out the rhythm of the dance between priest and council, but not without some toe stepping.

The issue of power surfaces when a board is placed in an advisory role. Each member receives some satisfaction from being selected to sit in on deliberations that affect the church. But only those willing to accept and go along with the power alignment will remain members of the board.

Often an advisory board exists as much for support as for counsel. The board generates personal, financial, emotional, and spiritual support for the church or the pastor. The council member who prays for a highly visible leader may receive the payoff of being close to the center of information and action. For some, that is enough, even if their power is minimized.

Political culture. A litmus question: *What group(s) or individual people in the church rely on you to carry and voice their interests before the board?*

Some church boards or councils are structured and constituted by representatives of particular groups or people responsible for particular program areas. When we asked board members how they came to say yes to being on the council, some replied, "By default"; they said yes to leading a particular function in the church and accepting that function landed them on the council.

When members represent the interest of particular groups or ministries, they will inevitably defend and protect certain turf, ensuring that budget, staff, communication, and recognition interests will be protected and promoted.

The culture of the board becomes characterized by negotiation—transactions that involve compromises, trade-offs, and accommodations. The board is forced into a delicate balancing act to keep the peace—while fostering the overall mission of the church. At times the peace is strained and even broken. Conflict management may then consume the energies of the board.

One church board that had just emerged from an extensive redevelopment project decided that members of the board could not serve on any other committee in the church. The board wanted to listen to and love the people, tend to their own spiritual formation, maintain oversight of the ministries of the church, and "vision" the future. Tense, burned-out board members were freed to see the whole forest and not just the individual tree that each had been tending!

Broker culture. A litmus question: *Who owes you a favor that you as a member of the board could "cash" for the benefit of the church?*

I once pastored a church in an aggressive midwestern agribusiness town. Many church members were local leaders. They served on numerous boards and projects in the community. Over the years some of them had accumulated "favors due" by helping others out in response to requests.

A suggestion was made to the church nominating committee that they look for board members among those who had proven themselves in the community as people who could get things done and might have some "chips" to cash for the church. When the nominating committee chose not to create a "power board," they left themselves open to the criticism of presenting a "weak" slate (even though their nominees had demonstrated commitment and leadership in the church and were spiritually sensitive).

Favor trading was one way the community leadership worked. This local culture subtly crept into the church even though few could consciously name it.

Bureaucratic culture. A litmus question: *Who stands to lose if you reorganize?*

Webster says a bureaucracy is "characterized by specialization of functions, adherence to fixed rules, and hierarchy of authority. It is a system of administration marked by red tape, officialism, and proliferation." A bureaucrat is "one who follows a narrow, rigid, formal routine or who is established with great authority in his own department."

Everyone detests bureaucracy, yet its subtleties often creep into the workings of church boards.

This can come about through attempts to "cover all of the theological bases." Committees are appointed in the categories of theological "oughtness." We ought to worship; we ought to do evangelism; we ought to educate our children; we ought to pray; we ought to tend and care. Board members settle into these boxes that seem theologically correct but may actually work against wholeness, concentrated efforts, priorities, and the ways people naturally gather or learn.

My presbytery has more than thirty committees. They are all well intentioned, missionally correct, and theologically based. People on the committees have a deep sense of calling. But like Gulliver we are restrained from action by countless tiny lines that are firmly staked down in theological and missional turf.

The bureaucratic model is supposed to be marked by specialization and efficiency. Unfortunately, overspecialization actually blocks efficiency.

Bureaucracy stymies a church board in a second way: in the identification people have with their positions. He is Mr. Evangelism or Trustee. She is Ms. Educator. People find affirmation and gain visibility via their positions in specialty areas, then emotionally feed on status. We have not discovered enough healthy ways to affirm and celebrate people in our church systems. An unhealthy bureaucratic system serves that need very well.

I note with interest the number of denominational leaders who have ridden a cause or issue into prominence in the church and then secured themselves in and fed upon the position gained.

Managerial culture. A litmus question: *What program area are you responsible for in order to carry out the mission of this board through other people?*

As a congregation grows, more and more program specialization will emerge. Board members are often recruited for their managerial abilities or specific ministry expertise rather than for their general spiritual wisdom. The board table becomes a coordinating ground for the programs each member manages. Resources, calendar planning, and communication become paramount concerns.

In this setting the pastor functions as a coach, knowing each assignment for each managing council member and how all the pieces fit together. That pastor becomes a mentor, director, cheerleader, and problem solver.

The program divisions may have their own teams, some with professional staff. Each program becomes a little congregation of its own. The total church functions somewhat like a cathedral in relation to its parishes. The pastor is to have a bishop's eye, seeing where to encourage, admonish, and celebrate. The church within the church will develop its patterns of worship, care, and providing resources for its own constituents.

Corporate culture. A litmus question: *What failure would be intolerable for this church?*

The corporate culture bears heavy influence on the church, primarily since many church board members are drawn from the corporate world.

Corporate culture places a high premium on growth, success, outdoing the competition, making a profit, surviving, and measuring and quantifying everything it does. Corporate-run boards run the risk of ignoring or devaluing the needs and well-being of their own people—honoring the "bottom-line" value over the value of people.

A corporate-culture church board is tempted to worship at the altar of growth and success—purported indications that the gospel is being proclaimed and lived. Conversely, numerical decline or an experience of failure implies that the gospel is not being proclaimed.

When decisions are being made, the underlying issue is not "What is faithfulness to God in this situation?" but rather "What will ensure growth and maintain stability and security?"

The pastor becomes the CEO personified, charged with creating a winning team, inspiring the faithful, and sailing the ship of success. When those things are not happening, the board sees its responsibility faithfully discharged by removing that CEO and finding the right replacement.

The pastor and board of First Church in Bartlesville found ways to transcend the corporate mentality. During one of our conferences, they gleaned new insights about "little things that make a big difference." When they went home they consciously inserted these little practices into their board meetings to create community and maintain a theological and spiritual focus.

Two years later I visited and evaluated that board. You'll remember that during their two-hour meeting they made only four decisions. But there was so much more going on! They laughed together fifty-two times! I went away with the impression that their culture was not "executive board room" but "happy family."

Strategic culture. A litmus question: *Do you know where you are going, and do you have a plan to get there?*

Over the last two decades, many churches have invested heavily in strategic planning and management by objective. Some of the processes have been useful; leaders need to look and plan ahead. But in recent days those efforts have waned. What happened?

During the last three years, I have conducted numerous board retreats early in the year as boards were being formed. My aim has been to develop a corporate quality to spiritual leadership. After we get started I frequently note a sigh of relief from the group. Once when I probed this sigh, I discovered relief that they would not have to paper the walls with newsprint and write ideas and consolidations of one- and three-year goals and strategic plans. They were weary of that effort because nothing much seemed to come from it.

I have also been interested in the predictions for the church made by "futurists" at the turn of each decade. Ten years later when we looked back, we often saw that some unanticipated event or unplanned opportunity emerged that dominated the energy of the church or nation in ways that no one could have imagined.

The culture of strategic planning assumes that we can create our own future. Theologically there is reason to believe that the future comes as a gift from God that we are to discover, participate in, and celebrate. Sometimes our plans can even turn into a new form of "works righteousness." We fool ourselves into thinking that if we can design the future and make it happen, we have proven to ourselves and others that we are right and good and Christian. But, as Bonhoeffer says, God will not allow us to live in a "wish dream." The only basis for true community is the grace of Christ that comes as God's gift.

Parliamentary culture. A litmus question: *Is this matter "out of order"?*

The parliamentary method, reinforced by *Robert's Rules of Order,* has been a useful way to consider agenda in an orderly manner. A deliberative body is able to make a decision and move on without getting tied in gridlock or paralyzed by a vocal minority. The method is, however, highly rational and stakes out adversarial positions "for" and "against."

As useful a tool as it is, parliamentary procedure also contains liabilities for faith communities. It does not allow for the wisdom that can come from nonassertive, nonverbal people or from those whose wisdom is more intuitive and takes time to emerge. The process "rushes to judgment" with little space for prayerful patience. Silence is not at home there.

Also, if the parliamentary method is the only arena of interaction for a deliberative board, people's conversation, anger, ego stroking, affirmations, and doubts will all have to pass through that sieve. That is asking too much of it. A win-lose result will not generate the embrace and support of the whole body. Many will be left on the outside.

. . . But Be Transformed by the Renewal of Your Minds

In contrast to being *conformed,* which so frequently means being fragmented and blown apart, being *transformed* means being healed or brought together as a whole. It is a metamorphosis of the board.

Corporate spiritual formation involves disciplines of the faith and the intention to place oneself alongside others in those disciplines. Formation comes through the ongoing daily process of the renewal of the mind. In describing this gradual process, a spiritual director proffered an image of water dripping on a rock. Eventually the rock takes on a shape through the effect of the water. It is not discernible from day to day, but practiced over a period of time, the effect is obvious.

The disciplines of scripture reading, silence, prayer, meditation, and contemplation can be corporate acts for boards. Through them we seek the mind of Christ. Paul asks the church to have the mind of Jesus Christ, who "emptied himself, taking the form of a servant" (Phil. 2:6 RSV). Seeking the mind of Christ as a board will produce certain fruits and behaviors that will become graces in the development of the whole church as a community.

> Be of the same mind, having the same love, being in full accord and
> of one mind. Do nothing from selfish ambition or conceit, but in hu-
> mility regard others as better than yourselves. Let each of you look
> not to your own interests, but to the interests of others (Phil. 2:2–4).

Servant leadership is not a weak, self-effacing posture. It is a
strong, positive image deeply rooted in a board's self-perception as a
community of value that is loved and gifted by God. We want strong
boards and councils of servants with the capacity to lead out of the integrity of who they are.

The Set Apart Lay Leaders project has been characterized by observers as a transformational endeavor rather than a pure research project. We have an agenda and want to make a difference. If it is truly
transformational, it cannot rely upon a few gimmicks and a set of mechanical procedures. The transformation must happen at a profound
spiritual level. I can't think of a level more profound than the renewal
of our minds via the "mind of Christ." Every board needs a center. Here
it is.

. . . So That You May Discern What Is the Will of God

Spiritual "sight" is the key attribute of the prophets. They were the
"seers of Israel" who were to discern the will and movement of God and
speak to the ordering of the nation's life in accordance with that will.

A primary task of church boards is the hard work of discernment.
Prayerful discernment is one of four practices in our model for the integration of spirituality and administration. (See chapters 3 through 6.)
After we'd spent two years building the four-part model, one of our
board- and council-meeting observers noted that "prayerful discernment
feels like the weak link." I would agree. Much work needs to be done in
this area.

But the terrain is slippery. Paul says as much. In Romans 11 he
says that the wisdom and knowledge of God are unsearchable and in-
scrutable. He questions, "Who has known the mind of the Lord? Or
who has been his counselor?" (v. 34).

Paradoxically, Paul asks us to discern God's will and yet suggests
that it is beyond us. We stand on the edge of mystery and peer into many
gray and shadowy areas, yet we are asked to try.

We like to be in control and in charge. But discernment is hard to program. The mystery takes us into an uncertain wilderness. But we must be willing to enter that wilderness to encounter God's will and ours. There is no easy way around it.

Or perhaps we have been "burned" by people who were sure they knew God's will. The pages of history are strewn with false prophets.

Or maybe we have been so preoccupied with seeking "God's will for my life" that we have missed the bigger picture. Some think God has a kind of "master plan" for each individual and life is a game the object of which is to find the master plan.

The process of discernment will be developed more fully later in this book, but for now let me say simply that the emphasis should be on seeing what God's will is for the world.

The prophets saw the *shalom* of God and recognized its implications for living righteous lives before God and just and compassionate lives before their neighbors. Jesus saw the kingdom of God—a wise and loving rule of God. Paul saw God uniting everything in Jesus Christ. This was God's big plan! The board that can get the big picture of God's will for humanity and this world will have a more accurate reading on God's will for the church or for the individual board members.

While pastoring a church in a steel town in Pennsylvania, I heard a conversation between two workers. One was very effective in all sorts of ministries and made a real difference in the lives he touched. "What is your secret?" he was asked.

He replied, "Every morning I get out of bed by installments. I am not very healthy, and my knees hit the floor first. With my knees on the floor and my elbows on the bed, I might as well pray. So I pray this prayer: 'God, I love you. What are you up to today? Let me be a part of it!'"

That kind of confidence that God is up to something big every day in my life (our lives) can get us started. Then we need a purging of all of the distractions and false gods. Following that, we center on the character and attributes of God, especially on the big picture. Then we probe and search *together* for God's leading in this situation. Finally, we put it to the test of the heart, testing time, community, and inner spirit to see what is of God.

. . . What Is Good and Acceptable and Perfect

God's will is good for all. For the church, for the world, and for us. Yes, we resist and fight God's will. That seems to be our nature. But unquestionably the board wants to do good. The prospect of accomplishing meaningful work for the good of the church shows high on the expectation charts of people entering into service on a council.

Think about the good. Paul suggests that the Philippian church should think about "whatever is true, whatever is honorable, whatever is just, whatever is pure, whatever is pleasing, whatever is commendable (Phil. 4:8). How will a board discipline itself to ponder until these rich concepts can penetrate its very fiber and being? Doing so is too often considered a waste of time. Or is it assumed that individual board members do this as homework and background preparation for a meeting?

Discernment is *acceptable* to God. Paul uses the word a second time in the span of two verses. The first time was in reference to the offering of a living sacrifice. This time it is in reference to discernment. Since God's ways are not our ways and God's thoughts are not our thoughts (see Isa. 55:8), we need to shift gears.

Discernment that is acceptable to God is done in a frame of reference consistent with the gospel, the cross, suffering love, and servanthood. This is not the world's wisdom, which prizes efficiency and advantage. But it is consistent with offering placed on an altar. Discernment is perfect, seeing things whole. To be perfect means to be complete. All the components are in place, even though there may be some warts, idiosyncrasies, and blemishes.

Let the church board, with all its baggage, with all of the contamination of society's culture, with all of its limitations, become the kind of leadership community that can see a vision of wholeness and direction. Only discernment of God's ways, revealed in the wide and long scope of Judeo–Christian tradition, can render a picture that stretches and compels.

Vision

The vision is clear. Although the church can learn to use many of the insights from the social and managerial sciences, it cannot adopt any one of them as its basic organizing principle. The organizing and enlivening spirit of the board of a faith community must spring from its own rich gifts and religious heritage.

Picture the 350,000 church boards and councils across America functioning with an agenda of worshipful work. Imagine their board members being transformed by the indwelling Spirit. Picture meetings inspired by the Spirit that in turn provide inspiration for the whole church!

Implementation: Ways to Plan an Agenda

Many new board members expect board participation will be an opportunity for personal faith development only to find a long, parliamentary-ordered, business-as-usual meeting. While asking for bread, they felt they had been given a stone.

"Stonelike" boards are those that do not attend to personal needs and aspirations. Stonelike boards try to make too many decisions. Dr. Tom Savage, president of Rockhurst College, observes that most boards can make only one or two good decisions in a given meeting (perhaps in a year!); considering this, adequate time and attention should be given to the really big issues over a span of meetings. Stonelike board meetings are repetitious. Stonelike boards are seduced into acting as a committee of the whole in response to incomplete committee reports or half-baked recommendations. Stonelike boards rely upon and are partial to assertive, verbal, and left-brain-oriented people. Stonelike boards rush to judgment, making decisions with inadequate lead and reflection time, with inadequate information, and without prayerful discernment. Stonelike board meetings may be cut and dried, with the real decisions having already been made by the pastor or staff. Board members are left with little power to act or lead.

"Breadlike" boards allow for bonding and trust to build as a community of faith is formed. Breadlike meetings are centered and focused by scripture on images of God and the people of God in community. Breadlike meetings take the time to prayerfully discern God's leading and call. Breadlike boards have farmed out many operational decisions, entrusting them to other people and groups that have been empowered and commissioned to act. Breadlike boards look at the "whole forest" and to its future. Breadlike meetings integrate inspiration with governance and feel more like "worship" than "meeting."

One pastor observed that board members, looking toward adjournment, tended to "check off" each report, wondering what time the meeting would be finished. He saw committee chairs animated while making their own reports but lethargic and passive during other reports. Commitment and energy were funneled into long-standing emotional and financial turfs. The structure of the meeting discouraged shared "visioning."

Careful consideration in planning the agenda for a meeting is every bit as important as planning for worship. Like the communion table, the board table should be viewed as "holy ground." If a meeting is to be worshipful work, with great potential for energy and excitement, much care needs to be given to its planning. A casual editing of last month's agenda makes for more stale bread.

Here are some suggested approaches:

Replace Committee Reports

Replace the litany of committee reports with spiritually rooted practices. The Set Apart Lay Leaders project is constructed around a four-practice model.

Story telling or history giving. Allow a portion of the meeting to surface these in general or in relation to a specific occasion or issue.

Biblical and theological reflection. The master stories from scripture, when woven with our stories and reflected upon theologically, will produce a center, a basic purpose, and a focused mission for the church.

Prayerful discernment. Decisions are to be "discerned" with a spiritual eye rather than through a rational or deductive process.

"Visioning" the future. Take the long, unhurried look. Anticipate the fulfillment of trends as well as the intervention of God through the unexpected.

These four practices create the potential for an integration of spirituality and administration. They do not need to follow the same order in each meeting. Nor do they require an equal proportion of time. Sometimes one practice is more appropriate to extended gatherings or retreats.

A committee may feel threatened as these practices are instituted. But that need not be the case if they can see that an agenda can easily be grouped into stories, reflections, decisions, and future planning. This framework can actually save an enormous amount of meeting time. The board is able to focus on what is most pressing, pertinent, and important.

Create an Annual Agenda

If a board or council can make only a few good decisions in a year, ask, "What is the most important decision that we have to make this year?" Pick the two to four major decisions and develop a process for consideration that ensures good communication, lead time, and prayer.

The rhythm of the church and program year lends itself to a planning cycle in which committees may need to report only once or twice a year, certainly not at every meeting. Their reports can include basic policy recommendations or future plans.

Prepare a Consent Agenda

Prepare a consent agenda in which all recommendations are in writing and listed together on a single page (or more). This should be in the hands of board members several days before the meeting. At the meeting separate out any items for which people request discussion or debate. Remaining items can be approved with common consent.

Some churches are more comfortable with an informal agenda that may not be in print. In this case, the presider can use a chalkboard; at the beginning of a meeting, ask members to identify stories, recommendations, or future explorations. List on the chalkboard any action items. Rank them in order of importance for consideration. This ensures that the board will give its best energies to the most significant decisions.

Create an Agenda Tracing Worship Themes

Create an agenda that traces the themes of the Sunday morning worship service. This method ensures that elements of worship, including prayers, hymns, affirmations of faith, centering in God's Word, offering, commitment, and blessing, are present.

Incorporate Prayers

Incorporate provisions for a variety of prayers that thread their way throughout the gathering. (See chapter 1 for suggestions.)

Reflect on the Meeting

Make provision for one of the participants to offer concluding reflections on the meeting. Reflections are not a recap of the meeting like oral minutes but a commentary on the process and significance of what has happened. *What really happened here, and what is the significance of it for our life together and for the church?*

The reflections may be pastoral. Often people stick their necks out in a meeting and risk more than they had planned to. They may feel uneasy and apologize, "Maybe I shouldn't have said that." The meeting's reflections might bless and affirm such a person's participation by identifying how helpful it was to the process. Naming the tensions, conflicts, or frustrations while affirming the board's resolve to hang together and be there for each other (as well as trusting God's sustaining grace) continues the pastoral role.

This reflecting role, which can be rotated through the group, raises awareness of the dynamics of board process and reduces the need for subgroups to conduct their own postmortem in the parking lot afterwards!

Work with a Design Team

Invite a design team of several board members to work with the pastor in framing the agenda. Board members can rotate through the team. This move would further empower the laity and ensure ongoing feedback on whether they are ingesting stones or savoring bread!

PART 2

The Sum of Its Parts: Four Transforming Practices for the Agenda of Meetings

CHAPTER 3

Coming from Somewhere: The Practice of History Giving and Story Telling

A Story:
Central Church Celebrates Its 150th Anniversary

Central United Methodist Church, located in midtown Kansas City, Missouri, near a university campus, had flourished over the years. Strong pastoral and lay leadership were hallmarks of its identity as one of the denomination's flagship churches. In recent years the church had pioneered in ministries to senior citizens. But as the congregation grew older, new pastoral leadership steered the church to look at its future.

As the 150th year of ministry neared, the church made plans for a year-long celebration of its rich history to honor the memory of its leaders. A series of inspirational events was scheduled. A contemporary music concert, a requiem, a men's glee club concert, visits of several college choirs, and a line-up of nationally known speakers filled the special-events roster.

Regular worship services featured the witness and stories of members on their faith journeys. A commissioned play depicted the key events of the church over its 150-year history. (It took eighty pages to cover 1844 to 1939.)

A smaller group went to work on a "Vision 2000" report to present to the administrative board. The report would point the way into the church's future. The opening statement focused on "spiritual enrichment and . . . a servant role," with special attention given to leadership. Since the pastor and a core group of leaders were already seriously discussing the establishment of a center for spiritual formation, they recognized the timeliness of being involved with a project that would integrate spirituality and administration.

After reading the "Vision 2000" report, I challenged this church:

The consideration of such a weighty vision must be done in the
context of a board which is spiritually prepared to wrestle with it.
There is a difference between a "strategic plan" and a spiritually
focused vision. Our project could help by giving your board a
framework and language with which to vision the future and make
decisions rooted in biblical, theological, and spiritual soil. The
board must wear or embody the vision in order to be credible. When
you say "spiritual enrichment and servant role," I ask, how will the
board embody that? If they cannot model in their internal life what
they vision for the congregation, the whole vision will collapse. The
emphasis on leadership means you will need to live it out in the
board as well as in the staff and in other lay ministries.

The board entered into a covenant with the Set Apart Lay Leaders
project to work together in a mutual learning effort. The church board
spent a full day in an orientation retreat. A major focus was their history.
A large, life-size mural depicting the history of the church dominated one
end of the fellowship hall. The mural's painter took the board on a verbal tour of her work. It revealed ministries among the pioneers who
docked at the Missouri River and prepared to go west on wagon trains.
The first church building, built in 1852, served as a hospital during the
Civil War. The founding pastor is shown preaching to the first five
members who sat in the shade under a large oak tree. A steamboat was
iced in during 1857. The women of the church took advantage of the
situation by holding a bazaar on the ship, making enough money to pay
off the mortgage on their five-year-old building. They viewed this event
as an "omen" from God.

The church's witness in every facet of a growing city's life was
condensed before our eyes. During the Civil War, both Southern and
Northern sympathizers contested church space, even drawing guns to
hold one another at bay. That bit of history was especially noteworthy
since the reunion of the North and South branches of Methodism took
place in Kansas City in 1939.

Over the years the church had moved, merged, or built a new facility
five times—on average every twenty-four years. Excitement, movement,
and commitment characterized the transitions. Now it had been twenty-
eight years since a major effort, and the church was lapsing into "fade

out." The church leadership recognized the need for a spiritual movement to continue the story line and marshal excitement and commitment.

Throughout the day-long retreat members told both personal and
institutional stories. Those who gathered entered into a vision of doing
board differently. As we prepared to leave, one member remarked that
he was sorry that six "power" members of the board had been absent.

A Master Story: Moses Tells Jethro All
Exodus 18:1–27

Jethro, Moses' father-in-law, approached Moses after he and the people
of Israel had escaped out of Egypt. Jethro brought Moses' wife and two
sons to him in the wilderness, near Sinai, the "mountain of God."

> Moses went out to meet his father-in-law; he bowed down and
> kissed him; each asked after the other's welfare, and they went into
> the tent. Then Moses told his father-in-law all that the Lord had
> done to Pharaoh and to the Egyptians for Israel's sake, all the hard-
> ship that had beset them on the way, and how the Lord had delivered
> them (vv. 7–8).

This relationship was a very special one. Some years earlier as a
refugee in the desert, Moses had met this "priest of Midian." Moses
married one of Jethro's daughters and, being part of the family, tended
Jethro's sheep. While tending sheep, Moses was called by God through
a burning bush. Having shared meals around the fire together, the two
men must have discussed the unusual experience and its meaning for
Moses. Jethro knew a desert spirituality and may have been a spiritual
guide for Moses; at least he blessed the mission of Moses to Pharaoh as
Moses departed.

After the confrontation with Pharaoh and the Israelites' miraculous
escape along a route across the wilderness and through a marshy sea,
Jethro wanted to hear the story directly from the lips of Moses. So this
private time in the tent was special. Moses told all—the ups and downs.

Jethro was delighted with what he heard. He blessed God, declaring
that now he was sure that the Lord God was more powerful than all the
gods in Egypt.

He offered a sacrificial meal and invited all the elders of Israel to eat bread together with him in the presence of God.

The next day Jethro noticed something that troubled him. Moses was judging the people from morning to evening. He was wearing himself out and all the people with him. Jethro then gave Moses some sound advice. He suggested that Moses divide the people into smaller groupings and appoint able, God-fearing, honest, and trustworthy people to administer over the groupings.

> So it will be easier for you, and they will bear the burden with you. If you do this, and God so commands you, then you will be able to endure, and all these people will go to their home in peace (vv. 22-23).

Reflective Story Weaving

The master story blesses Central Church's story in the common pursuit of an authentic spiritual dimension of life. At the burning bush, Moses was introduced to "I AM"—a personal God who willingly enters into relationship with humans. In desert spirituality, three impressions surface to those who place themselves into extended silence. (1) They come to realize that God is personal—coming to human beings offering a name and a relationship. (2) They come into solidarity with the suffering of the world. Note Moses' awareness of the pain of Israel in Egypt. (3) They are faced with a call to do the work of God in the arena of the suffering.

Central Church has a grand Methodist tradition of direct, immediate experience of the Spirit of God. You might even say that a powerful brand of spirituality is genetically encoded in the denominational DNA. Wesley and Jethro could have held some interesting conversations!

The master story confronts Central's story as well. Central is an energetic program- and activity-centered church. Its people are busy about many things outside as well as inside the church. Some found an appeal in retreating to the desert of reflection and story telling, but others resisted and avoided the opportunity. Jethro met with all the elders for his retreat meal. Central's attendance record can't match that.

The master story nudges Central to move in some new directions. They face the distinct challenge of finding a way to excite and commit the congregation without constructing a new building, relocating, or merging with another congregation. I commend their attempt to find this exciting new direction through an extended celebration and visioning process. The church recognizes the "DNA" story line that has shaped its history; it is trying to stay within that good heritage while moving to a new level of witness and ministry.

A priestly account of Moses' life from Exodus 6 indicates that God appeared to Moses' ancestors Abraham, Isaac, and Jacob as El Shaddai (God of the Mount), not as Yahweh (I AM). But to Moses God was revealed in the burning bush as Yahweh. One has to ask where Moses' spirituality was formed—in Pharaoh's court, at mother's knee, or in the desert?

It is tempting to view Jethro as a forerunner of the early-church desert fathers and mothers, casting him in the role of Moses' spiritual director! A spiritual director is not a teacher or counselor, but one who stands alongside another, listening and paying attention to the inner spiritual movements in the experience of God. Moses' burning-bush experience could not have been a momentary "flash" accompanied by immediate new insight and life-changing directions. I see Moses returning over and over again in his mind to the experience and sitting by the fire discussing the matter with Jethro for hours on end before finally coming to some distilled wisdom about it. Jethro may even have introduced Moses to Yahweh. At least he certainly is interested in knowing the exodus story and how Yahweh has been involved.

Moses' respect for Jethro (he bowed before him), their genuine friendship (they inquired after each other's health), his regard for Jethro's priestly function (he made sacrifice and offered a meal), and his heeding Jethro's administrative advice add up to a very special and unusual father-in-law/son-in-law relationship. Too often people think about this story only in terms of administrative and organizational theory. But that view is much too limiting. A thick sublayer of spiritual exploration and reflection underlies it all. This foundation of genuine spirituality is the key to leadership and administration.

Summarizing the distilled wisdom from the story weaving, we would observe: (1) The spiritual life is a journey, filled with both hardship and reward. (2) A personal God with a name desires to enter into personal encounter with people. (3) The desert is an arena for spiritual self-examination, listening to God, conversion, repentance, and change. (4) God's presence and power can be seen in the events of people's lives. (5) God's call to special leadership engages one with real pain and need, sometimes drawing the leader into the structures of power and/or into unjust systems. (6) God will find a way to work around or even through our human inadequacies and excuses.

Discerning

As parents of four children, Joyce and I wanted them to know their rich heritage so they could create their own identity. We camped with them on the grounds of an old castle in Scotland that bears their mother's maiden name. They played in bunkers on the bluffs overlooking the North Sea in Denmark and heard stories of their Viking ancestors. They visited a lighthouse constructed on the site of their great grandfather's birth. They visited churches and examined records of their faith ancestors. When Daniel Boone came up for study in American history, they took the family tree to school to "prove" they were his direct descendants. We told them as many stories as we could about their good heritage. We are pleased with the many ways in which our sons and daughter have reflected this identity. They know from whence they came.

Stories do that. They provide a wonderful sense of identity. One's faith journey is constructed by a series of interlinking stories of events, moments, relationships, and impressions in which God's presence is evident.

Faith is a journey with a story line. The story line for the effective board member is very personal, for its background is the member's own faith story. The individual has a story—a faith journey. So does the congregation. Our ability to hear and grapple with stories in the congregation springs from the tap root of their connection with our own story. If awareness of the presence of God does not permeate our own personal story, we're unlikely to detect God's hand at work in the stories of the congregation. Coming clear about that creates an identity that is indispensable to effective leadership in a faith community.

Christ Presbyterian Church in Edina, Minnesota, developed the practice of opening each monthly board meeting with a faith journey story from one of its members. Members knew well in advance when their turns would be and made serious preparations for their presentations. When the members owned a conscious identity as people of faith in relationship to God, they could proceed out of that identity in all they discussed and decided. Members that we interviewed reported that these stories were a highlight of the meeting, anticipated by all.

Stories build community. Pity the council that has no time for personal stories. They ignore and shut out a vital source of life. They try to govern by "the facts" without listening to the inner experience and feelings of their colleagues. Without a foundation of community, the work of a board will be severely crippled.

This is especially true in the board's function of discerning and visioning. With great success one presbytery used a discernment method in its member churches. When the presbytery tried to use the same approach with its own council, the effort failed because the council was not "a community."

Stories produce life and energy for a board meeting as well as identity for the storyteller. In observing a five-hour segment of a presbytery meeting, I was struck by the unusual amount of energy and enthusiasm that peaked in this deliberative body. Toward the end of the afternoon, most were tired; some had left early. Then it happened. Within a fifteen—minute period, I observed laughter, tears, and applause. Then I realized that we had unconsciously moved away from a planning and announcement mode into story telling. Three stories had been told that did not appear on the planned docket. The stories were energizers for the whole body!

How is a community to know how to pray for its members if no information is passed along about needs, fears, hopes, and joys? A body is formed; it does not just happen. Leaders of boards need to allow time in retreats and meetings for members to use some first-person pronouns to connect with one another. Leaders dare not assume that because board members know the "duties of their office," they are automatically formed as a group with a high level of trust and deep caring for one another.

Whenever community and identity are threatened or lost, the way back is through stories. During the exile in Babylon, when Israel lost its national identity along with the symbols of the temple and the city that reinforced it, the people gave attention to stories. After a period of great grief and consternation ("How can we sing the Lord's songs in a foreign land?"), they gathered and organized the stories that went back to their founding days with Abraham. They remembered. They literally re-membered—became a people again. Synagogues were formed as centers for story telling, teaching, and wisdom gathering. Congregational elders emerged who were more than village wise men or tribal power brokers.

The rabbis taught and the elders governed with wise rule.

A recent collegium on board development identified story telling as the most prevalent and workable practice in our model to integrate spirituality and administration. In our discussion I expected to move on to explore the other three practices. Instead, the group stayed with the subject of story telling. I wondered if this signaled an avoidance of the harder and more elusive aspects. Or was it that people simply do what they know how to do? Perhaps *story* was so important and vital to them because denominations and congregations are in a period of redefinition and reformulation. More than ever, stories are a source of transformation.

Stories also invite commitment. When one's personal story is woven with the institutional story—affective, loving relationship surfaces. Dr. Richard Chait of the University of Maryland was involved in a study that attempted to identify the characteristics of exemplary boards and trustees. The study focused on boards of private colleges. Exemplary trustees from exemplary boards were interviewed. The dominant trait could be summarized in this statement: "I just love this school and believe in what it is doing."[1]

Board members often carry on a quarrel in their heads with the institution they govern. If it is a lovers' quarrel, the institution will be well served. Several years ago I took a group of elders to visit the meeting of the General Assembly of the Presbyterian Church. Over breakfast we had an extended conversation around the subject of "our love for the church" and from whence that love came. I was amazed to see the amount of weaving of personal and institutional stories. Commitment to the church grows from the interwoven stories.

Trustee-development projects in not-for-profit boards have taught us the importance of knowing the history of an organization. Congregations also have a faith story—a corporate one. They have a rich, deep history that speaks but often is not heard. Often the history that is probed is only a thin, recent crust.

Congregations have histories that are distinct and unique. They are rooted in biblical images, bathed by centuries of tradition and beliefs, honed in the grit of encountering alien cultures, and styled by the gifts and visions of the saints who live on in the memory of the people.

One cannot assume that a congregation can be typed by denominational affiliation alone, although that is a powerful indicator. Each congregation develops its own story, ethos, and personality. James Hopewell made a major contribution to the field of congregational studies when he identified that each congregation plays out in scriptlike fashion its narratives or story lines.[2] Whether or not a congregation's story fits into a classic narrative category, it is unique.

The founding story is all important, for the congregation will play out that myth in both conscious and unconscious ways.

Saint Margaret's Episcopal Church of Lawrence, Kansas, one of the Set Apart Lay Leaders' covenant churches, is a new church development with only a three-year history. The planners, being schooled in congregational development and family systems theory, were intentional about creating a founding story. They organized a cluster of small groups that gathered together for unusual and lively celebrations. The power of those early events, gatherings, and stories would shape and drive the church into its future.

Second Presbyterian Church of Kansas City, Missouri, was organized in 1864 as an antislavery church. Over the years they have had a rich history of marshaling the resources of the congregation for ministry in the city. I led their church officers in a review of their story, asking them to identify the formative people, ministries, and events of their life span. After a thorough review of their founding and subsequent stories, I asked if they could identify any threads that ran through their time line. One responded, "It seems as though we have throughout our history a streak of holy belligerence! We seem to be at our best when we are joining forces to stand over against something." Another added, "It's like it's in our genes!" Another said, "Yes. That's our DNA!"

Just as the Avis Rent-a-Car story line is "At Avis, we try harder," Second Church might say, "At Second, we stand over against." They are still playing out their founding story. To be effective, the church board must know this story and its power—not only in the living memory of the church but also in its day-to-day existence.

The people who write histories often miss the "thick" history. They are seduced into using the construction and destruction of buildings or the coming and going of pastors as the organizing structure for their story.

A thicker, more authentic history will tell the story through the group's "defining moments." Village Presbyterian Church in Prairie Village, Kansas, experienced nearly fifty years of history under one organizing pastor. As the board told its story, members went to the events (many unplanned) that were defining moments for them. These moments provided a window through which to review the character of the church and its leadership. Thick history will reveal the laypeople who have been influential in the life of the congregation—the people who embody the vision and character of the church. They make up the great "cloud of witnesses" whose voices continue to be heard. When I am working with boards, inviting them to identify these people, I often ask board members to tell me about each person and then compare perceptions.

Carl Dudley observes that churches have three kinds of members: (1) The socializers, who attend and support the activities of the church. They are the easiest to replace. (2) The organizers, who plan and lead the ministries of the church. They are more difficult to replace. (3) The symbolizers, who bear in their being the character and ethos of the church. They cannot be replaced. They are the saints who live on in the memory of the congregation.[3]

A thick history will review the ministries born and cultivated—perhaps also those put to rest—over the life of the church. How did they come to be? Who bore the vision in each ministry? Who was deeply affected or even changed by their participation and involvement—and how? What biblical images energized and drove the ministry? What unique gifts were called forth in people who made it "go"?

A thick history will unpack the events: What really happened there? Duncan MacIntosh, a staff member for the American Baptist denomination in Valley Forge, Pennsylvania, conducts story-telling events for congregations. He invites them to relate a recent event that has had a significant impact on the congregation. Then they unpack the story by surfacing various impressions of the story. Who were the players? What were their feelings? What roles were they playing? Over a span of years, Duncan has made a significant observation: Congregations that mention God as a player in the story tend to be congregations with vitality; they often are growing. Those that do not mention God (later stating, "We just assumed God was a player") tend to be lethargic, often in decline. MacIntosh concludes that something about naming God as an everyday player in their conversational stories gives permission for members to witness. They obviously believe that God is alive in their midst, and visitors who come to them pick this up. Conversely, visitors pick up the absence of God in the living memory of the other churches.[4]

Jethro's probing of Moses' account of the exodus deliverance was centered on the activity of Yahweh. He nailed it for all generations since and to come: God did it. Yahweh delivered them! No congregation's history is complete without naming God's role in its story.

"Here I raise my Ebenezer. Hither by Thy help I've come" is a line in "Come Thou Fount," one of the great hymns of the church.

"What is an Ebenezer?" people ask.

It's a pile of rocks. When Israel crossed the Jordan River, they were instructed to pick up twelve stones from the bed of the river and stack them by the riverside. Why? So that when people (especially children) passed by and asked, "What do these stones mean?" they would be told the story: "Here God helped us!"

A church I served declared an Ebenezer Celebration Day. Each member was invited to bring a rock that was significant for some personal reason. The rock was to signify a way in which God had helped that person. At an appropriate time members stacked their stones in the churchyard with verbal testimonies of God's help. Some of the accounts were personal, using first-person pronouns. Other accounts were corporate, using plural pronouns. People witnessed to the ways in which God helped them as a church.

It's okay to jest about the "skeletons in the closet." But it's vital to let every church board know about the Ebenezers in the churchyard and to give them the codes to decipher the deeper witness to the presence of God in their stories.

Denominational traditions add to the thickness of local church history. Our Set Apart Lay Leaders project has gathered a network of participants from across a wide spectrum of church traditions and has provided a language with which to engage one another's experiences and dreams. A recent collegium included Roman Catholic, mainline Protestant, evangelical Christian, and Jewish participants. While relishing mutual discoveries and experiences, they held deep respect for the uniqueness of each tradition.

Our observers of board meetings reported that, although they were aware of the denominational labels of the churches they visited, the board members seldom made references to their own heritage. A few exceptions popped up. Catholics referred to Vatican II and the defining moment of moving the altar away from the wall. Presbyterians referred to their *Book of Order* and to some of the foundational principles it contained. Methodists mentioned Wesley's criteria of scripture, reason, and so forth. Disciples pointed to the ministry of the laity but were often trying to figure out how to make best use of the elders, who were only a part of a larger administrative board. Lutherans incorporated the Protestant work ethic into the board character. More study needs to be done on how each tradition consciously or unconsciously conditions the process of governance. We see some differences as outside observers; board self-awareness is another matter.

Another slice of the thick history can be seen in "moments" each board member has experienced. When I work with boards, I ask each member to identify a "moment" in which they were moved or touched in some profound way—to tears, to laughter, to wonder, mystery, or awe, to ecstasy, or to deep pain or embarrassment. Weaving their stories of "moments" with one another and within the larger congregational story can be insightful.

In one board of a seven-year-old church, two-thirds of the members made reference to the same "moment." Narratives ran like this: The congregation was gathered on the Sunday before Christmas for a special service of worship and music. The six-year-old son of the choir director was to sing a solo with the accompaniment of the adult choir. Everyone in the congregation loved this cute little boy with the pure voice. When the time came for him to sing, he stood up in front of the congregation and provided their first common moment—of inspiration. Then, in his excitement, he then and there provided their second common moment—by vomiting. They were embarrassed with and for him. The third common moment came when his father, the choir director, lifted him into his arms and lovingly embraced him.

As board members reflected on this story, they saw it as a window through which to review their common life. This new church provided euphoria and excitement for the young, newly joining families. It was a place where they could take risks and even fail, showing their real humanity. And it also was a place where they experienced the outstretched and loving arms of a God who embraced them through it all!

Let boards see the rich, thick history of their congregations and the complex, yet profound evidences of God's gifts of community and grace. They really are sacred spaces ready for exploration.

Vision

My vision is clear enough. I see history giving and story telling as a vital and legitimate part of the meeting agenda of boards and councils. Not all agree. Many boards see it as a waste of valuable time that could be better used, considering the real issues before the board.

So many boards are future oriented—making plans for coming events and ministries, then figuring out a way to enlist people into them. They rarely have time to review the stories of what has happened, make sense out of them, and learn from them.

I see boards composed of people who have identified and can communicate their own personal faith journeys. I see councils forming close relationships of trust. I see a board developing its own story line and moving forward together as the people of God. I see councils taking unhurried time to mine the rich and thick history of their congregations. I see board members reviewing aspects of history related to a particular issue they are discerning. I see a council seeking out stories from members and groups within the congregation. And I see history and story as a legitimate agenda for any meeting.

Set Apart Lay Leaders project, in cooperation with Presbyterian Research Services in Louisville, conducted a survey of 605 elders from across the country who had completed a term of office. One question asked about the place of stories in their meetings: "How often did each of the following events or actions take place while you were on the session?" We listed fourteen optional choices. Stories ranked at the bottom of the fourteen.[5]

	Often	Sometimes	Never
Share faith stories	15%	54%	31%
Review church stories/history	11%	54%	31%

We also asked, "Would each of the following make serving on the session more meaningful?" Again we asked for responses on fourteen topics. Responses for faith stories and church stories ranked eleventh and twelfth on the list of fourteen.[6]

	Yes	No
Share faith stories	68%	32%
Review church history/stories	58%	42%

More than one-third do not think stories and history have a place in the agenda of the meeting. Perhaps they recall insignificant or unrelated stories from past meetings. Perhaps they cannot imagine how stories could add to a meeting. Perhaps they feel threatened by the prospect of using first-person pronouns in relation to their own lives. Or perhaps their board has not learned the fine discipline of reflecting theologically on its stories.

Our experience with boards and councils with which we work has also identified an element of resistance. From observation we have seen that "resisted" stories are generally those that take a lot of time and seem to have no relation to the major concern of the agenda. One church used half of the meeting time on Bible study and sharing, leaving participants with mixed feelings about the stories.

One evaluator summarized,

> Most of the meetings also incorporated history giving and story telling into the agenda. But it seemed sort of "superimposed" on the meeting, not really an integral part of the life of the board. The moderator led the group through a history-giving exercise, but it didn't hook into the rest of the agenda. The history giving that came up spontaneously, as members wrestled with an issue . . . was integrated into the agenda because it dealt directly with the topics at hand. I don't think it "works" to do history giving for its own sake.

First Christian Church, Topeka, Kansas, experienced some initial resistance from members of the board who were in legal and government work. As the meetings for this large board of ninety opened, the members were divided into table conversation groups for Bible reflection and story telling. The pastor recently related how much better the meetings were going. When I asked him what they were doing differently, he said they had reduced the size of the board, eliminated the table talk, and had invited presenters to relate specific stories. Some of the stories were integral to a report being made on behalf of a committee or other church group. The stories were touching, having an emotional "punch." The whole board was able to experience them together. Some former "resisters" were more positive about these recent meetings.

Boards should seek stories that stretch members in their views. Arnold Smit, a Dutch Reformed pastor from South Africa, explored our model and the place of stories within it. He warned, "In South Africa we have been telling stories, reading the Bible, and saying our prayers. But they led us astray. We only listened to the stories from the center of our life. We needed to hear the stories from the edge." Prophets (as well as heretics) stand at the edge. A board needs to sound a prophetic voice. Stories from the edge can inform that voice, even if we are inclined to resist them.

At that same collegium, Mennonite historian Dr. Robert Kreider, an invited respondent, summarized:

> Much attention was given to story telling. It is helpful to include different kinds of stories: (1) my story—which may be at its best when it is sliced into small pieces; (2) our story—that is, our congregation, our denomination with its gifts and its limitations; (3) your or their story—a parallel or contrasting group or peoplehood story (to help liberate us from our natural ethnocentricism); and (4) the story—the Christ story and the biblical story. For faith and fellowship building in the church council, the need is less for the polished storyteller than for a receptive climate where it is easy to share. Perhaps even more important than the gift of story telling is the gift and art of inviting forth sensitively the stories of others.

Implementation

Our learning-covenant boards used stories twice as often as boards with which we had not introduced the model. Giving orientation and training and legitimizing stories on an agenda can make a difference.

Whom to Call?

When looking for history, "who ya gonna to call?" Our research shows that a board looks to a pastor 38 percent of the time for historical information that has a bearing on the council's work. But they look to a colleague on the board 57 percent of the time. Boards need to identify people who carry memory and can inform them; boards need to affirm these people in that role and call forth their gifts. One of the casualties of the rotary, limited-term-of-office system that most churches employ is the much needed corporate memory.

Mr. Brown is an eighty-five-year-old "elder" who sits on the council of Fountain of Hope Lutheran Church, a neighborhood storefront church with multiracial membership. He is not regularly elected but sits on the council because he is recognized by the community as an "elder" with wisdom and memory.

Some years ago he walked out of a congregational meeting being run with a heavy hand. Others followed him to the parking lot, where they decided to begin meeting in their own homes. That fledgling group became the organizing nucleus for Fountain of Hope Church. Mr. Brown plays a vital role. Every board needs its "Mr. Browns"!

Suggestions

Here are some suggested ways to tell stories in board or council meetings:

Invite to a meeting one to three congregational members who "bear the history" of the church. Interview them, requesting that they all offer their memory and observations about a particular "slice" of history or specific event. Allow them to interact and generate the story together as one reminder leads to another. They might also reflect about how this event influenced them personally and what meaning they perceive it has for the congregation.

Take time to look into the historical antecedents and threads of influence when considering an action step. When the lessons of history are not available, boards repeat mistakes of the past without knowing what they are doing.

Plan a church-wide celebration of a particular historic event or ministry. Draw in many participants; bring all of the story data to the board table, where you can work as a team. Select a symbol that characterizes this event.

"Group tell" a story or event in the life of the church, preferably one that occurred since the last board meeting. This can be done by each person giving a small piece of the story, introducing it with the connector "and then. . . . " When one is aware that an aspect of the story is missing, the connecting words can be "but before that. . . . " The moderator or one familiar with the story should start with "at the beginning. . . . " Include people, their expectations, reactions, and ongoing impact.

Draw a time line of the history of the church. This device has been used very effectively by Trustee Leadership Development in training consultants to help not-for-profit organizations know their history. I am adapting it here for use by church boards.

Place two long tables end to end and cover them with white table paper. Draw a line lengthwise and mark the years by decades. Invite the board members to record their names twice below the line—once when they first came to be associated with the church, and a second time when they began service on the board or council of the church. Have them record above the line the names of people in the church who have been influential to them or others. Are there any spiritual "wisdom figures" there? What was the nature of their wisdom or influence? Are there any anecdotes to be told about them?

Record below the line any significant events or program ministries. Be sure to include "founding stories" and "defining moments." Write above the line any events in the larger culture or church that have had an impact on the congregation.

Place exclamation marks where the group or individual members were "touched" or "moved" in some way. Place a bumpy line where things were difficult. That is an important part of the story to which boards tend to close their eyes. Naming and clarifying those troubled times can lead to healing and reconciliation with the past.

Request all council members to write or organize their faith stories. Provide helps for them, perhaps in the form of organizational hints, such as "when my life took a different direction"; "when I changed my mind"; "when I saw things in a new light"; or "when God was more than a word to me." Then schedule those who are willing to present their faith stories at the beginning of each meeting (one per meeting).

Invite individual people or small groupings to come to the meeting and tell the story of an experience or event. They will be affirmed and grow by telling the story; what's more, the board will grow by hearing the tale. The story can become a focus for prayers and reflections. People, for instance, who have been touched in some way by the ministries of the church can tell about that impact, express appreciation, and practice the recital of "testimony" with integrity. The story needs a "blessing," which the board can give by listening and responding!

Offer opportunity for all board members to identify an occasion since the last meeting when they were aware of God's presence or activity in their own lives, in the church, or in the larger world community.

Give board members an opportunity to relate the story of a "moment" since the last meeting when they have been moved or touched by an experience in the church.

People love to tell and listen to stories. They are a necessary and legitimate component of the agenda for any meeting. When the stories are processed in theological reflection, people are able to distill their core values, beliefs, and meanings, and to celebrate the common faith they hold.

CHAPTER 4

Distilling Wisdom:
The Practice of Biblical and
Theological Reflection

A Story: Westminster Church Baptizes Mikey

In a retreat setting, the session of Westminster Presbyterian Church in
Saint Joseph, Missouri, was invited to identify one congregational story
within the last year that had made an impact on the group. They were to
retell the story with as much detail as possible, including every board
member's perception of it. They selected the baptism of Mikey, a
twelve-year-old mentally handicapped boy whose foster family was
uniting with the church in membership.

At the session meeting when the elders were authorizing the
baptism of two of the family's natural children, one elder casually asked,
"But what about Mikey?"

What about him?

After considerable discussion of the meaning of baptism and with
the guidance of the *Book of Order* and the creeds of the church, the
session decided to interview Mikey, his foster family, and his natural
mother. After those conversations, they met and agreed that Mikey held
a simple love for and trust in Jesus, that all of his "parents" would be
supportive of his faith journey, and that he should be baptized.

On the appointed day for his baptism, the congregation was caught
off guard when Mikey burst into a loud, joyful laugh as the water ran off
his head. Then they were deeply moved to see his smile as he beamed
his way up the aisle during his presentation and introduction to the
congregation!

This was a powerful and defining moment for the church. Fifteen
years earlier they had initiated a ministry to the parents of mentally
handicapped children without imagining something this deeply touching
would happen.

When the session members completed telling their extended story, which included a number of corrections and additions, they were led into a period of biblical-theological reflection upon their experience of Mikey's baptism. When they were asked to think of a biblical story or theme connected to Mikey's story, they settled on the account of the baptism of the Ethiopian eunuch from Acts 8.

They read the story over several times, observed a brief period of silence, then allowed the two stories to interact. Finally they listed some concluding learnings, meanings, and faith affirmations. The whole process, from story to meaning, had taken them ninety exciting minutes. It was 10:30 p.m., yet the people were so turned on by the process that they asked their pastor, skilled in the art of theological reflection, to lead them through another story and study. That reflection lasted until midnight!

A Master Story: Philip Baptizes a Eunuch
Acts 8:26–39

Then the angel of the Lord said to Philip, "Get up and go toward the south to the road that goes down from Jerusalem to Gaza." (This is a wilderness road.) So he got up and went. Now there was an Ethiopian eunuch, a court official of the Candace, queen of the Ethiopians, in charge of her entire treasury. He had come to Jerusalem to worship and was returning home; seated in his chariot, he was reading the prophet Isaiah. Then the Spirit said to Philip, "Go over to his chariot and join it." So Philip ran up to it and heard him reading the prophet Isaiah. He asked, "Do you understand what you are reading?" He replied, "How can I, unless someone guides me?" And he invited Philip to get in and sit beside him. Now the passage of the scripture that he was reading was this:

> "Like a sheep he was led to the slaughter,
>   and like a lamb silent before its shearer,
>   so he does not open his mouth.
> In his humiliation justice was denied him.
>   Who can describe his generation?
> For his life is taken away from the earth."

The eunuch asked Philip, "About whom, may I ask you, does the prophet say this, about himself or about someone else?" Then Philip began to speak, and starting with this scripture, he proclaimed to him the good news about Jesus. As they were going along the road, they came to some water; and the eunuch said, "Look, here is water! What is to prevent me from being baptized?" He commanded the chariot to stop, and both of them, Philip and the eunuch, went down into the water, and Philip baptized him. When they came up out of the water, the Spirit of the Lord snatched Philip away; the eunuch saw him no more, and went on his way rejoicing.

Reflective Story Weaving

What is biblical–theological reflection? Let me offer an illustrative comparison. One of my favorite television news commentators was the late Eric Sevareid. As Pogo would say, "HE SPOKE IN CAPITAL LETTERS." Sevareid was always eloquent and insightful. After his colleagues had presented twenty minutes of news of the day, Sevareid would do five minutes of news "commentary." He would summarize one of the salient news items, then go back into our national, cultural, or even religious traditions to lift out a precedent or principle. He may have quoted one of the founding fathers or great leaders. Then he would conclude by saying, "Therefore it is important for us as Americans to remember that . . . " or, "We now value in a new way . . . " or, "We will now intend to. . . . " In a way Sevareid was story weaving. He set up a dialogue between the news of the day and the tradition that is our heritage. After allowing today and yesterday to speak to each other, he concluded by isolating values, beliefs, and purpose for all to see. It was as if he were underlining the distilled wisdom.

Sevareid's practice was very close to that of biblical-theological reflection. For the faith community, the Tradition may dialogue with future visions, current issues, or recent stories. We will begin our exploration with stories.

Many laypeople who serve on boards are reluctant to enter into biblical-theological reflection because it seems to presume on the role of the professional theologian, the seminary-trained pastor. Laity may feel shut out when the pastor jumps in to offer the already worked-out theological conclusions. They may feel intimidated by the pastor's professional aura. Or they may feel inadequate, not knowing enough about the tradition to venture a thought. But I am suggesting that theological reflection is the prerogative of every lay leader. Increasing numbers of pastors are developing the abilities to help groups process theologically in their own settings rather than giving them the textbook answers from another setting.

Boards need to liberate the Bible from its imprisonment in the "opening devotions" of the meeting. Those devotions, wedded with an opening prayer, form one of the bookends that routinely hold committee reports together. (Besides, to be a bit cynical, it provides a time cushion for some to arrive late, just in time for the "real meeting" to begin.) The Bible and a hymnal may be used at any point in the agenda, especially when stories are told.

With the understanding that theological reflection is the province of the laity and that biblical reflection can be integrated into the agenda of a meeting at any point, let us return to the stories at hand.

In terms of Mikey's baptism, Westminster Presbyterian was in for a surprise. The Spirit was about to pull a fast one on them, just as with Philip in the Acts account. Philip's successful preaching ministry in Samaria was interrupted by the Spirit's instruction to go down south along a well traveled highway. The elder who asked, "What about Mikey?" likewise diverted the thought-train of the session.

A strange set of circumstances brought Philip and the eunuch together in the same chariot. Likewise, a strange set of circumstances brought Mikey, his foster family, and the session together. "What about Mikey?" drew the session into biblical and theological reflection, for they were forced to deal with the question on a level deeper than religious ritual or common expediency. The eunuch's question, "Look, here is water! What is to prevent me from being baptized?" also went to the depths.

The eunuch had been reading from Isaiah. Philip picked up on this and started where the eunuch was—scripturally but especially emotionally. One subtle aspect of the story lies in the purpose of the eunuch's trip to Jerusalem. He had gone there to worship. Even though he held high public office as the secretary of the Ethiopian treasury, he would not have been permitted to enter the temple area because he was "not all there." An incomplete human being according to Jewish law, he was considered unworthy. Imagine his humiliation!

The passage he was reading included the words, "In his humiliation justice was denied him" (v. 33). He asked Philip if the prophet was speaking about himself or about another. Was the eunuch reading himself into the story via his own humiliation? This makes for interesting speculation at the least. I would love to have heard the full conversation! Philip starts with the eunuch's own personal situation, brings in the fuller scope of scripture, connects it with Christ, the suffering servant, who was also humiliated, and then announces the good news about Jesus.

In the weaving of these two stories, the biblical story actually blesses Westminster's story and provides a number of touch points that give insight into the ways of the Spirit.

One gets the impression that the Spirit was initiating in both situations, while both the session and Philip were responding in ministry.

The common notes of joy in and around baptism are too good to miss. Mikey laughed his way up the aisle of the sanctuary. The eunuch went on his way rejoicing. Meanwhile, the session has turned back to business, and Philip is heading back up north to preach the good news. What a fascinating interlude or interruption the Spirit provided for each!

From these stories the following wisdom can be distilled: (1) The Spirit of God is an initiating evangelist. (2) The use of scripture will point to Christ. (3) Ministry responds to the Spirit's initiative. (4) Deep listening provides a connecting or starting point. (5) Grace is accompanied by infectious joy.

Many boards spend so much time planning future events that they fail to look at the past. They need to unpack the stories in their midst and learn from them as they surface meanings and identify their core values and faith principles.

We encourage an extended time for history formulation in retreat settings, but story telling in regular meetings is equally vital. Reflecting biblically and theologically upon stories can follow a simple six–step process:

Step 1: Select a significant story. If it occurred in the life of the congregation, invite the whole board to retell the story using the connecting words "and then . . ." or "but before that. . . . " If it is a personal story, listen closely. Fellow board members should be able to repeat back what the person said to his or her satisfaction.

Step 2: Unpack the story by identifying the people involved along with their roles and feelings. Also identify other people or groups affected by the event.

Step 3: Capture the essence of the story by selecting an agreed-upon symbol for the story.

Step 4: Connect the story with scripture—a story, person, theme, verse, or image from scripture that comes to mind. This could be called the master story. Read it and fix it firmly in the group's collective mind. (The group may also want to tell the master story using the recall method cited previously, "and then . . . " and, "but before that. . . . ")

Step 5: Weave the stories together. Allow group members to interact. James Hopewell suggests a way this can happen: When the biblical story is laid alongside our individual or collective narratives one of four outcomes can be expected. (1) The biblical story will bless or affirm our story. (2) It will contradict or confront our story, standing over against it and judging it. (3) It will lure, tease, or entice the story to move toward change. It will nudge it off dead center and barely begin to turn it in a new direction. (4) It will transform the story into something new.[1]

Step 6. Isolate and identify meanings and beliefs in light of this experience of story weaving. What is really important to you? What can you now affirm? What now is your primary purpose?

My experience in working with this model reveals that stories energize boards. Some boards take as long as an hour to tell all the facets of a story. But resistance may crop up when the board is invited to identify a scripture that connects with the story. Most fear they do not know enough about the Bible to make it work. I suggest that they start with what they already know. Once they get started, they'll be surprised at the amount of collective memory they really have! They'll also dig out the Bibles and find aspects of a story they were previously unaware of.

Discernment

Dr. Don Shriver, president emeritus and professor of applied Christianity at Union Theological Seminary in New York, served as the theological consultant at our 1994 collegium. He observed:

> The meeting revealed many of the strengths of your fourfold program for joining spiritual life to administration in congregations. You took story telling, Bible study, prayer, and the struggle for discernment seriously in the process of the meeting. I think that there is general agreement that your most important discovery is the importance of story telling. There is less clarity, I think, on

how prayer and Bible study are integral and natural to the deliberative processes of a congregational board, but the claim that church decisions must be contexted by these elements is strong and persuasive.

My surmise is that local church boards will need a lot of patient guidance and encouragement by ministers if they are to become genuine deliberative bodies in matters theological. I still hold to the concept of the minister as "teaching elder." But I think we train ministers in seminaries better for the proclaiming of faith than for the exploration of faith. And, even when [clergy] give ourselves to the role of explorer-leader, we may not know how to deal with the anxieties of lay leaders about the openness, the uncertainty, and the controversy that may have to characterize theological dialogue in our time. Keeping the right questions alive in group deliberations from month to month can pose a lot of threat to nonacademic folk in the church. They may not always appreciate the importance of keeping such questions alive. Even when formulated, consensus answers are hard to come by. We wouldn't have so much clash between liberals and evangelicals in the church if we had more patience to hear each other out and to hear questions out of the Bible and out of contemporary life to which no one has adequate answers.

A related concern, raised several times in the meeting, was how personal stories, Bible study, times of prayer, and proposals about the divine will can be kept from being intimidating and smothering to dialogue in meetings of church boards. The *theological* question and reflection could become the necessary antidote to this danger: as when anyone on a board raises a question like, "Who in the New Testament is our best model for leadership in this situation? Peter? Paul? Gamaliel?" And a question like, "What is the Spirit telling us in the great variety of theological viewpoints assembled in this congregation?" No one seems to be classic Presbyterian or Lutheran or Catholic anymore! When laypeople become comfortable with questions like this, we may find that they are, at least for particular occasions, the real theologians. I want church leaders one and all to be theologians and not to be shy of the title. Moses is the model here: "Would that all my people were prophets!"

The introduction of the Bible should begin discussions, not end them. This is particularly true when the Word stands in relation to current issues before the council. Many sensitive issues or opportunities present themselves to a board. They call for patient and prayerful discernment of God's will and call. Scriptural grounding, probing, and guidance become important practices along this path. Removing the Bible from its imprisonment in bookend devotions and introducing it in relation to one or more important issues in a meeting can lead to some profound and challenging—and difficult and disturbing—decisions.

Here is a step-by-step process a board could use until biblical-theological reflection becomes more natural for them. It is illustrated by the story of a meeting of the Parkville Church board, which attempted to follow the process.

Step 1: Identify a significant issue for consideration. The board of Parkville Presbyterian Church chose "Covenant to Care," a proposal from its presbytery, to enter into a covenant to care in a special, self-determined way for victims of AIDS and their families.

Step 2: Look at the many sides of the issue and how it "comes close" to the lives of each board member. The discussion leader told two personal stories of a family member and a friend who had died of AIDS. He then invited others to tell their stories. The board expected to hear only a few rare and distant stories—and perhaps one from a physician on the board. They were surprised to hear that every member had a story to tell and shocked to learn how close the stories were.

Step 3: Select a scripture passage that may or may not be related to the issue. The Parkville Church board selected a passage suggested in the background materials accompanying the covenant request—the story of the Good Samaritan.

Step 4: Ask yourselves three questions. These questions are drawn from a powerful little book authored by Walter Wink, *The Bible in Human Transformation*.[2] (1) What does the text say? Just get the story out as it is. (2) What does the story mean? Look at its context and relation to other biblical material. (3) What would it be in me/us? Picture it in your setting. Parkville Church board centered on ways they "pass by on the other side" in avoidance patterns and on the call to "take care of him," reviewing their own style of care giving.

Step 5: Returning to the issue under consideration, can you identify any new "twists" or insights? Parkville's board quickly saw that their AIDS-related stories must be the tip of an iceberg. Surely the congregation along with them was sitting on a number of unrevealed and untold stories. They all had been unwittingly involved in a conspiracy of silence. Before any further steps could be taken, the session needed to allow the stories to come out and minister to people who carried deep wounds and fears. They decided to schedule a Sunday morning worship service with AIDS as its theme and to "prime the pump" for stories. In worship the board members would tell their stories as they had around the table that night.

Scripture had encountered them in the context of the meeting's agenda. Reflecting biblically and theologically was not an empty but an engaging exercise.

The four parts of the Set Apart Lay Leaders Project model are interconnected and interrelated practices. They are not four gimmicks that can be drawn from a grab bag and used in isolation. Stories go somewhere and lead to the naming of meanings and values. Biblical and theological reflection produces a central driving purpose that will inform decisions to be discerned and visions to be followed.

In a consultant-training program exploring the importance of clarifying an organization's purpose, I suddenly saw that the process was applicable to any organization, even a twisted organization such as a racist-supremacist group; the process was value neutral or amoral (not immoral). This prompted me to ask where authentic values and purpose comes from. It is here that "traditioning" enters the picture. The values and purpose of a faith community must be rooted in and tested against the best of its long-standing traditions. These include scripture, creeds, hymns, art, and historical experience, all of which point to wisdom. The fruit of the good process of biblical-theological reflection will be a good mission and purpose.

Robert J. Schreiter affirms the importance of creating theology within the culture in which the community of faith lives rather than borrowing it or importing it from another culture.[3] Many missionary efforts have imposed theologies, often with saddening consequences. But the base communities from Latin America arc illustrations of theologies that have listened to their own culture, considered the tradition, then affirmed their own faith in that context. In many ways boards are creators of "local theologies" in their month-to-month reflections on the tradition's encounter with their own agenda.

Vision

The process of biblical-theological reflection produces some basic beliefs and a focused purpose that drives the present but also projects into the future. Whether a board is taking an extended retreat to look far and wide into the future or considering what they see "coming down the road" in the context of a regular meeting, the need for a solid biblical foundation is crucial.

Tom Sine, in his book *Wild Hope,* warns us against creating pipe dreams or proving our self-worth by following the plans we make. Sine offers a scripturally based, four-part schema that reminds us that God creates the future.[4]

Step 1: Identify your preferred vision of the future. This follows the projection of our basic beliefs and values into a new and future setting.

Step 2: After consideration of a scripture passage, ask, "What image or character of God is presented?"

Step 3: Ask, "What image or character of the people of God in community is presented?" (Faithful? Servant? Witness?)

Step 4: Identify the way or path to that future. We are not to charge forcefully or blindly into the future, says Sine. Instead, we are to proceed in concert with the character of the people of God and in the light of the image of the very One who creates the future and offers it to us as gift—the God revealed in scripture.

I have a vision for the placement of Bibles at each setting of a board table, just as one expects to find them in pew racks in a sanctuary. The Bible is not to be used for "proof" of tightly held visions of the future or as a proof text that supports a cause. But when used to fathom the image of God and God's people, its power to inform, reform, and transform is significant. We are a people of the Book and should not apologize for introducing it into the formerly not-so-sacred board room.

One of the Set Apart Lay Leaders project's goals has been to establish the board table as a locus for individual and corporate spiritual formation. That is beginning to happen. Interweaving the people's stories, issues, and visions with the creative power of the age-old "master stories" provides the key to letting it happen.

Implementation

The sixteen churches with which we worked in the second year of the project were beginning to use theological reflection in their meetings. Two of our observers concluded that the pastors assumed the expected role of theological reflector and that little active reflection was done by the board as a whole.

But the other two observers saw theological and biblical reflection taking place in lay interaction.

In one meeting I observed, a number of affirmations of belief, meaning, or value were put forth in a very natural and conversational way. Most had some biblical image or reference attached. One lay member was very adept at articulating these, and the group received his gift as a helpful contribution.

Occasionally an affirmation was voiced in unison, building on or even creating a corporate consciousness. Several boards recited their own church mission statements as affirmations of faith.

Strategically speaking, the board or council is a crucial arena for congregational renewal and revitalization efforts. If the board can move beyond "business as usual" into the experience of active and energized faith, it will model and lead in ways that impact the whole church. If the board becomes a community of spiritual leaders, the church is bound to feel its effect.

But pastors often miss this golden opportunity, applying their energies to other ministerial functions. A recent study conducted by Christian and Saint Meinrad Seminaries—funded by the Lilly Endowment—discovered that among the long list of pastoral functions, administration and stewardship produced the least satisfaction and most frustration. The same study showed that pastors have not been adequately equipped in seminaries for these tasks. Yet when pastors chose their continuing education programs (you guessed it), they avoided administration and stewardship, opting for courses and seminars that concurred with pastoral functions in which they already felt competent![5]

I want to challenge pastors to turn their many talents and gifts to the vital and exciting ministry of administration. A concentrated focus on the board and council can provide a great deal of satisfaction for the pastor and affect the congregation in many surprising ways.

Some pastors are already moderators of empowered boards. Their developmental edge is to focus the meeting to integrate spirituality and administration so that faith, both individual and corporate, will be formed at the board table.

Some pastors exercise a strong hand of control, using the board as an advisory panel. For them the developmental edge is sharing leadership and empowering laity in the ministry sanctioned by their baptism.

Still other pastors are on the sidelines while a lay president, chair, or moderator quarterbacks the meeting. For them the developmental edge is to resource, support, and collaboratively plan life-giving meetings.

No matter what a pastor's structural relationship to the board may be, some common pastoral roles cut across church traditions and organizational frameworks.

Visionary

A new paradigm is emerging for board meetings. It has a simple elegance. It draws on the roots of deep traditions in faith communities rather than from the board cultures in the society at large. It integrates spirituality and administration. It enlivens meetings and inspires participants. It may be described as "prayerful gathering" or the "work of worship." To maintain its vitality, any group must have at least two people who hold a vision for the group. I will venture to say that for a board one of the two must be the pastor. Glimpse the vision. Select a symbol for that vision. (Meshing gears is one possibility.) Then let that new way of seeing and being "board" align everything that is planned and done in the name of the council.

Gatekeeper

Having a unique position in relation to the council, a pastor can selectively screen or advocate for information and visions. Any effort to change the culture of the board must have the ear, mind, and voice of the pastor. Without that active support, little positive change can be anticipated.

A pastor may see exciting possibilities but may block and resist them because he or she feels insufficiently trained or personally inadequate. To that person I would say: You are not alone. Help and resources are available. You stand on the edge of a potentially exciting journey!

Spiritual Director

As I was explaining our attempts to integrate spirituality and administration to Kay Collette, who heads the Program for Spirituality at San Francisco Theological Seminary, she interrupted to observe, "You are really doing group spiritual direction!" She may be right.

Spiritual directors are akin to the "seers" of Israel. The pastor as spiritual director is one who has an awareness of the movement of the Spirit of God in the meeting and on the board members. When I do spiritual direction, I pay attention to two movements: (1) ways in which surrender, relinquishment, and letting go to God are happening and (2) ways in which taking hold, caring for what God cares about, and responding to a deep inner calling are taking shape. These same dynamics operate in meetings.

The spiritual director will also enable groups to reflect theologically on their stories, issues, or visions.

Mentor

The pastor most often assumes a pivotal role in the preparation and orientation of new board members. In that role it is important to clarify expectations and provide a clear presentation of tasks, operating procedures, freedoms, and boundaries. But the mentoring role does not stop there. It also includes active listening, accompanied by the posing of questions that help the council member probe deeply into meanings. The pastor's modeling can help to create a trusting and nurturing environment that permits honesty and inquiry on the entire board.

The pastor who is not moderating the meeting actually has the ideal perspective from which to view the whole forest, not just a few trees. Distance does afford a unique kind of wisdom.

Dialogue with board members in a one-on-one setting between meetings provides an opportunity to reflect and offer encouragement. This compares to the coach who, in addition to working with a whole team, often sits down with each player alone.

Architect

Too many boards wear themselves out by considering too much material in a given meeting. Designing a focused and inspiring agenda is one of the greatest gifts a pastor can offer the council. I would suggest the creation of a design team consisting of the pastor, the lay moderator or clerk of the meeting, and at least one other board member. This third slot could be filled on a rotating basis.

First, take the long view. What is the most important decision the board has to make this year? Plan a process over a span of months in which (1) the issue can be fully explored, (2) related biblical and historical bases can be touched, (3) ample time for prayerful discernment can be taken, and (4) a solid consensus can be built. Consider an annual agenda with given subjects to be considered each month.

Second, delegate or commission as many decisions and oversight responsibilities as you can to individual people or other groups, reserving basic policy, important new ministries, and future directions for the work of the board.

Third, build in opportunities for the board to become a community in which each person is valued and celebrated. Be sure to structure into the process various practices of worship and opportunities for inspiration.

Liturgist

As liturgist, the architectural function continues with the inclusion of elements of worship in the agenda. When the culture of a board is one of worshipful work or prayerful gathering, prayers, hymns, silent waiting, affirmations of faith, and biblical centering will thread through the meeting. Allow the worship to be closely related to the agenda being considered.

Politician

This term, of course, is used in its most positive sense. A skillful politician can mold people into a purposeful and caring community. A politician will work to ensure healthy relationships with constituent groups. In a congregation this may be the relationship of the board to the staff, to other groups in the church, to the community at large, and to the denomination. The creation of a trusting and safe environment where listening is practiced, where inquiry is invited, where information is shared openly, and where honest discussion precedes decisions—this is the work of a good politician.

Officiant

Some communions place the pastor as moderator of the board. The power and control of the pastor is not the issue. The real issue is the special place of governance at the board table in the ministries of the church. Just as the role of the pastor in the administration of the sacraments reinforces the unity of the church, the same high ground is seen for the board table. Both the communion table and the board table are to be seen as "holy ground."

Moderating a meeting of a faith community is not to be taken lightly or done casually. The pastor may stand at two tables, and both are equally important to the life of the church. Both are locations for faith formation and for proclamation of the gospel.

The board table is not a second-class table where only business transactions take place. It holds the bread of doing the will of God. That bread feeds the people around the table and the larger congregation as well.

Conclusion

I see many encouraging signs in these days as churches are seeking clues for a transformed future. Pastors are functioning less as theological answer people. They are more and more steerers of a process of theological reflection from a biblical base. In many ways the church is going back to the basics. Those basics can operate in board rooms of congregations. Boards, like basic communities in Latin America, can learn to read the Bible in light of their real experience and search together for meaning. That is the new task for leaders. Its process has been absent from many board rooms. Since the quest for meaning is the hallmark of leadership and since people are set apart for leadership on church boards, creating gracious space for biblical-theological reflection in the agenda of boards is essential—not optional.

CHAPTER 5

Seeing with Spiritual Eyes: The Practice of Prayerful Discernment

Two Stories about Church Councils

Discernment in Selection: Missouri Parish Selects a Council

Guardian Angels Roman Catholic Parish, Kansas City, Missouri, was in the midst of a transition. For years it had served a German ethnic constituency with a well-staffed school and church. Their priest had formed a parish council in the late seventies, but because the council began to micro manage the parish, the priest disbanded it seven years later. The parish went for six years without a council. After the priest left, the congregation again moved to form a council, thanks to the leadership of Brother Terry, a member of the parish staff.

The neighborhood was changing, with younger families and Hispanic newcomers. The parish was also changing. The school was set to close. The parish staff was headed by a female parish administrator instead of a resident priest. The new, ten-member council would play a new and different role in the life of the parish. They needed able, committed, and visible lay leaders to come forth.

The diocesan staff was poised to assist the parish in the council selection. This staff was impressed by the creative efforts of the Archdiocese of Milwaukee in pioneering a "discernment process" for council selection. Milwaukee's archbishop, Rembert Weakland, had said,

> One must be willing to be involved in that whole difficult struggle of discernment. . . . This means all seek to determine, not the easy solutions, but what will be the source of grace, holiness and growth to God's people. Unselfish love, willingness to sacrifice, care for

others, not personal ambition, become important. True discernment demands of all Christians that God and God's Kingdom—not self— be the center of concern.[1]

A five-week series of open gatherings was planned to discern the leadership for the new Guardian Angels parish council. People with leadership capacities and interest were encouraged to attend. Over the five-week period, a group of forty-eight to fifty studied scripture and prayed, considered the purpose and mission of the church, and explored aspects of the giftedness of the baptized. Finally, the discernment group participants were called together again to make specific selections from their own number to serve on the council.

This prayerful, open, searching process was related to the specific needs of the parish. From that process, ten council members were selected. In contrast to that of the former council, they were to be a vision group and not an administrative entity.

Discernment in Administration: North Hills Goes for Consensus

North Hills United Methodist Church in St. Louis recognized the need to revitalize its administrative process. Boards and committees were bogged down in parliamentary rules and scarred by the painful consequences of win-lose decisions. The board had a reputation for contentious debates, with people leaving the church after each fray. The board needed to capture the leading of the Holy Spirit in its meetings.

The church entered into an eight-week design to recapture the Ignatian process of spiritual discernment—for individual use and for the board and committees to use corporately. Their print resource was *Yearning to Know God's Will,* a workbook on "discerning God's will for your life" written by Danny Morris, staff member of the Upper Room.[2] More than sixty people went through the initial orientation.

To serve on the administrative board, the nominating committee selected people who had received this orientation in personal and corporate discernment. Subsequently a different tone emerged in meetings. Board meeting attendance has gone up by 33 percent. The board and all of the committees continue to receive training. The congregation is now enthusiastic about prospective service on the board.

This revitalized North Hills congregation has dealt with several major issues that with their former style of operation would have torn them apart. One was the introduction of a "Vision 2000" long-range planning report that included a list of recommendations that had been sensitively discerned over a three-month period. The changes were approved unanimously! The second issue involved a change of their fiscal year, departing from the conference's calendar fiscal year. The congregation's decision to buck the denominational grain evolved out of a patient consensus process.

All meetings now integrate worship with business. Chairpeople are comfortable in calling for silence in a meeting because the individual board members have experienced silence and value it.

Master Story

Discernment in Selection: Samuel Selects David as Leader
1 Samuel 16:6–13

Israel was in need of a new king because Saul's reign was no longer acceptable in God's sight. Samuel, the prophet, was instructed to go to Bethlehem to anoint a son of Jesse. When he laid eyes on Eliab, the firstborn of Jesse's eight sons, Samuel thought, "Surely the Lord's anointed is now before the Lord." Not so. The Lord said to Samuel, "Do not look on his appearance or on the height of his stature, because I have rejected him; for the Lord does not see as mortals see; they look on the outward appearance, but the Lord looks on the heart" (vv. 6–7).

One by one, seven of Jesse's sons passed before Samuel. All were rejected by God. Finally David, the youngest son, who had drawn sheep duty, came in. "He was ruddy, and had beautiful eyes, and was hand-some. The Lord said, ' . . . this is the one.' Then Samuel took the horn of oil, and anointed him in the presence of his brothers; and the spirit of the Lord came mightily upon David from that day forward" (vv. 12–13).

Discernment in Administration: David's Mind Is Changed
2 Samuel 7

King David was a builder. He made Jerusalem his new capital, con-structed a "house of cedar" for himself, and moved the sacred Ark of the

Covenant to a tent in the city. His next project would be to construct a
temple, a house for the Ark. Even Nathan the prophet liked the idea.

But a sleepless night changed Nathan's mind. Out of the stillness of
the night, God spoke to Nathan, objecting to David's building a house for
God. "No," said God. "I will build him a house!" The Lord promised
David a house that would be eternal, with a king to come after him who
would plant Israel as a secure people and reign forever.

David could have bucked the voice of God that came by way of an
inner prompting of Nathan. He was no doubt tempted to plunge ahead
with his own plans. He didn't. His prayer of response acknowledges
God's greatness and accepts God's promise. David admits that he is a
servant.

> For you, O Lord of hosts, the God of Israel, have made this revela-
> tion to your servant, saying, "I will build you a house"; therefore
> your servant has found courage to pray this prayer to you. . . . You
> are God, and your words are true . . . therefore may it please you to
> bless the house of your servant (vv. 27–29).

Reflective Story Weaving

Who were the prophets in our stories? Samuel and Nathan are obvious
picks. They listened to the voice of God, which seemed to speak so
clearly. Yet I doubt the decision was so easy and the voice so clear. I
see Nathan tossing and turning through an extended sleepless night until
the fuzzy voice and deep impressions became distinct. I see Samuel
fidgeting uncomfortably in the presence of old Jesse, who was eager to
show off his mature sons. Samuel could hardly have had peace deep in
his heart in the midst of this rush to judgment, and his struggle must have
been intense.

Once we lay aside the impression that God's speaking is in an un-
mistakable, bell-clear, and audible "voice," we can identify with these
prophets in our own struggle to hear and discern the voice and will of God.

Moving to contemporary times, Archbishop Weakland of Milwaukee is a "prophet" who saw something missing in church governance and
empowered lay leaders to develop and participate. His staff members,
who worked creatively and wrote their learnings for other councils, were
prophets. In the story of the Guardian Angels council, the staff of the

Kansas City Diocese carried a prophetic banner, introducing the parish to an idea never tried in this diocese. The parish administrator shared the new vision of lay leadership and graciously bonded together a multiply gifted new council. The council itself took some visionary risks, for the terrain was new to them. All prophetically refused to be content with business as usual, especially when they saw the damage the status quo was inflicting. Each demonstrated the capacity to listen with spiritual ears.

Eventually an entire parish council was oriented to the discipline of silent listening; when a moderator asked for silence, the group could make creative use of it rather than resisting it as a waste of time.

The nominating process at Guardian Angels was turned upside down. A new set of criteria was introduced in an effort to reflect what God looks for in spiritual leaders. Samuel was tempted to judge by what he saw on the surface—appearance, height, stature. Besides, Eliab was a firstborn—a natural leader.

Modern nominating committees may be tempted to equate physical height with spiritual stature. And they are vulnerable to being influenced by tangible factors, such as level of education (is a Ph.D. a better candidate than a high school graduate?); vocation (is a white-collar executive a better candidate than a blue-collar worker?); and connections (is a highly visible, well-connected public figure a better candidate than an obscure, private person?). When a nominating committee is advised to look for leaders who have spiritual sensitivity and theological awareness, they will stare blankly unless they have been schooled in discernment.

Members of Guardian Angels who participated in the discernment process of parish council selection placed themselves in a vulnerable position. Forty people in an open forum trying to select ten from their number opens the scary possibility of rejection. Opening one's heart to God via the scrutiny of human beings is risky business to say the least. Even David, the fearless shepherd boy, may have shuddered had he known what the stakes were!

When it comes to discernment in administration, the best plans that human wisdom could muster were laid aside by King David—and by the North Hills United Methodist administrative board. Both saw themselves in servant roles—acquiescing to the will of God and seeking God's presence and blessing upon their work. The openness to allow God to build a house rather than framing it for themselves was a mark of humility and faith.

The distilled wisdom from these stories reveals: (1) Outer, human

measurements and standards do not equate with God's criteria. Real
prophets see a larger picture from God's vantage point. (2) Prophetic
vision comes through struggle, discipline, and silence. (3) Our best laid
plans may not be God's will. We need to take the long view couched in
the promises of God. (4) Listen to the Spirit. (5) Attention to God's
Spirit brings blessings and calls. (6) Open-hearted servant leaders are
vulnerable.

Discernment

Our earlier consideration of Romans 12:2 introduced us to the concept of
discernment through the phrase "that you may discern what is the will of
God." Discernment is such an elusive and mysterious term precisely
because it presumes on the will of God. Who is any human being to
really know God's will?

Of the four practices in our model, discernment is the most difficult
to grasp. It cannot be reduced to a simple procedure. The Quakers have
worked at it faithfully for three hundred years, and they say they don't
have it down pat yet!

The term has historically been the property of the Quaker movement
and Roman Catholicism. The Jesuit order has majored in the disciplines
of personal discernment. Now the term is becoming an "in" word among
mainline Protestants, but it is being casually used to mean almost anything that has to do with a decision.

The Set Apart Lay Leaders' advisory panel wrestled with the term,
since it seems so difficult to communicate. One suggestion was to substitute *deliberation* for *discernment*. But deliberation denotes a rational
and deductive process that is too far away from the heart of discernment.
Another panel member suggested that the emphasis should be placed on
the word *prayerful* rather than *discernment*, emphasizing the listening
and receptive aspect of the concept. We even asked if discernment was
so rare and special that it only really occurs once or twice in a lifetime.
If so, it may not be germane to the ordinary work or the month-to-month
meetings of boards.

At the end of the discussion, I had difficulty giving up the word.
The depths that it probes in the individual and in a group contain rich
treasures, even though the probing itself may make us uncomfortable or
uncertain.

Perhaps the mystery of God's initiatives and our response to them is at the heart of it. We name this mystery "discernment," but we can't completely describe it or control it. The best I can do is circle around it a few times and offer a few hazy snapshots.

As long as the church adopts the practices of corporate decision making from the cultures of business, management, or politics, we have a pretty clear picture of the process: Get all the information. Consider the options. Know the consequences. Weigh the pros and cons. Reason your way to a conclusion. Communicate with clients, consumers, and colleagues. Debate the merits. Get on with the vote. Secure its implementation. Monitor. Evaluate.

But faith communities march to the beat of a different drummer. What is God calling this congregation to be or do? What is God's will for us now? These decisions are not so easily discussed and managed.

Discernment Is Not

We can talk about a few things that discernment is not.

Discernment is not to be equated with consensus decision making. We welcome the new openness that the consensus process brings, with more participation in, ownership of, and commitment to the decisions made. Consensus beats the win-lose approach that can polarize and divide. But Jesus was crucified at the end of a consensus decision. Humanity's reasoned judgment has limitations and can easily go astray. My Calvinist tradition teaches that humankind's capacity for self-deception is limitless!

Discernment is not a political process. Recently a national gathering of more than five hundred Presbyterians was called together to "Discern the Spirit." A denominational budget crunch precipitated the invitation. The consultant who led the open process (for there was to be no preset agenda) asked all to identify their passions—that which they felt most strongly about in the church. For several days they stirred around in their passions, finally passing on their gathered passions to a small "shape and form team"—sort of a Senate-House conference committee, but with five hundred bills to reconcile. When we start with "our passions," we are already into a political model that invites compromises and trade offs.

Discernment is not a logical, rational, ordered discipline that

leads deductively to inescapable conclusions. Sister Mary Benet McKinney, after working with school boards in the Archdiocese of Chicago, turned her attention to floundering parish councils. She observed that councils had "baptized" management models from the secular culture, but the models "didn't take"! Her book, *Sharing Wisdom,* reveals the place for discernment. She contends that every council member has a piece of the wisdom. The task of discernment is to allow that wisdom to come out. Assertive, verbal, and rationally oriented people need to be slowed down. People whose thought processes are more intuitive or pictorial need the chance to bring their wisdom forth. Parliamentary process seldom allows for that.

Discernment is not to be equated with making decisions. Former Jesuit Tad Dunne, after four years of marriage, reflected on the subject of discernment. He related that he could not identify a moment when he made the decision to marry. He had asked himself a lot of questions but kept probing around until he discovered the decision that was already there. It had been made in the depths of his being.

Discernment Is

Discernment means to "see" or to "know" or to "acknowledge" what is. It is to see the movement of God, perhaps only in the dust kicked up by the wind. It is to see from God's perspective. If this is so, then the discernment process is one of uncovering the decision—not of making it. The Spirit prays within us "with sighs too deep for words." As we listen to the Spirit, those prayers begin to surface into our consciousness. They may have been operating subliminally, like popcorn ads that could be flashed too fast for the human eye to detect in a movie theater but yield a craving for popcorn!

I spent one summer during my seminary years on an archaeological dig in Jordan at Old Testament Bethel. We were in search of walls— temple, house, and city walls. We were looking for pottery, tools, and layers of ashes. We did not go in with bulldozers. We did give the workers picks—but for scratching—not for swinging over their heads. The "real" work of archaeology was done with trowels and brushes. The whole process was one of carefully uncovering the tell (mound of ruins) to discover the treasures within it. Nothing was to be destroyed. Graves, walls, and implements were painstakingly unearthed and carefully photographed.

Like the archaeologists' trowels and brushes, the tools we use to "dig" for discernment are gentle: questions, silence, reason, dreams, and images. These enable the will of God to surface into consciousness or be discovered before our eyes. Boards are to stay with an issue, prayerfully uncovering all of the overlaid "stuff," until at last they "see" what God is up to, what God is calling people to be and do.

Paul states that all creation is groaning in travail, waiting for the revelation of the new people and new world that God is ushering in. This childbirth image reminds us how eager we are to see a newborn baby. After months of speculating about this mysterious new person forming in the hidden recesses of its mother's womb, at last we are able to see the baby "uncovered" to reveal its size, gender, and family resemblances. The decision waiting to be "born" or uncovered through prayerful discernment is God's decision, planted at the deep places of our corporate destiny by the Spirit.

Ignatian Lessons

The Ignatian process of discernment holds lessons in corporate discernment for boards faced with decisions. The Jesuit practice is a bold one that comes with some built-in safeguards.

Corporate discernment assumes the practice of individual discernment by participating members. Each person needs to be grounded and centered in seeking God's will. Personal ego needs, which often drive groups, are to be laid aside.

Rigorous self-examination is the starting place. Individual members need to ask what they bring to the decision—both the light and the dark sides, both strengths and weaknesses. The group as a whole needs to ask the same questions. Story telling can reveal much about orientation and attitudes. This is a way to clear the air and provide a board with genuine freedom to see and decide.

Look at the life of Jesus or at images of God. Jesus' spiritual journey included testing, choices, and graces. Contemplation on the person and work of Christ moves boards to consider the choices they have made as they have been led by the Spirit.

Consider the call today. Seek to uncover it by asking questions. See it in the perspective of the kingdom of light or the kingdom of darkness. Go ahead and reason the positives and negatives. Weigh them. Reason is also God's gift. See where the group comes out. Has a decision been uncovered and discovered?

Let the decision sit. Put it to the test of time and to the test of the heart. Is there peace about it? Or does the decision lead to discomfort? Boards can make tentative decisions, then live with them for a while before finalizing them.

Discernment is a patient process. It cannot be hurried. Some important decisions have taken councils two years to uncover! Saint Mary's Parish in Colt's Neck, New Jersey, was bursting at the seams. They needed more space to accommodate their ministries and programs. The parish council was prepared to build a new multipurpose gymnasium, since that was what all the growing churches around them were doing. The priest asked them to slow down and put the matter to prayerful discernment. They did that for a period of two years and finally built a "spiritual life center." It's nothing like any Christian education wing I have seen, nothing like a retreat or counseling center, and nothing like a multipurpose gym. It is a unique building—yes, a spiritual life center! The center was built on the church grounds but separated from the office and worship buildings by a parking area. As I entered this hospitable space, I noted the number of quiet nooks where one could sit alone or with another in conversation. A small, colorful chapel beckoned. The consultation rooms did not position one person in power over the other. I could have spent two days in the library! I imagined several hundred people gathered for a festive dinner in the large assembly room.

The Churning Waters of Discernment

Consulting scripture, waiting in silence, and corporate soul searching are not an "easy way out." Efficiency-minded boards are accustomed to "controlling the agenda," but the discernment agenda tends to have a life of its own. It cannot be pushed and resists our efforts to manipulate it. Aslan, the lion Christ-figure in C. S. Lewis's delightful *Chronicles of Narnia,* is "not a tame lion." Neither is discernment. It's so precocious and so powerful and so difficult to corner that . . . well . . . that one would think that God is involved in it. That's just the point. And that's what makes it at once so terribly threatening and so wonderfully exciting.

For a group about to plunge into the churning, refreshing waters of discernment, here are some swimming lessons.

Be selective in the number of issues to be discerned. Thinking in terms of an annual agenda, that may mean only several significant decisions over the period of a year—certainly not more than one per meeting.

Begin with corporate and private self-surrender. Surrender, especially of the ego, is hard to do. We tend to hold on to our pet investments and our pride. "Not my will, but thine be done" is a corporate issue that rarely gets named. Jesus said, "Unless a grain of wheat falls to the earth and dies, it remains just a single grain; but if it dies, it bears much fruit" (John 12:24). Take time to name what needs to die before the discernment begins.

When I do spiritual direction, I look for two movements within the directee. One is the way in which a person is surrendering to the Lord—dying unto self or relinquishing the ego. I also look for ways in which the person is taking hold of God's call. Board meetings are like group spiritual direction in that sense. Tilden Edwards of the Shalem Institute observes that a deliberative debate or discussion that has gone longer than twenty minutes will be ego driven. He suggests stopping for two minutes to refocus.[3]

One test for corporate discernment is to ask if there is truly willingness and readiness to follow whatever leading may come.

Focus on core, scripture-based values and beliefs.

Gather information from many quarters and listen to one another.

Allow time in silence both at and between meetings for prayer and deep listening.

Come to agreement on what your common prayer will be. Jesus said, "If two of you agree on earth about anything you ask, it will be done for you by my Father in heaven" (Matt. 18:19). One of the boards with which we were working used the saying, "We are forming our prayer." They meant that they were agreeing on what their prayer would be—asking for what was beyond their reach. This became a prelude to making a policy or program decision.

Seek consensus in the decision. This is not always possible, but it is worthy of the effort. Under the presence of the Spirit and with the mind of Christ, the highest good is sought for the community through faithful response to God's call.

There may be times when consensus is impossible. In those times, it is important to honor those who dissent and to allow a way for dissent to be registered. The fabric of the group can then stay intact. The Quakers have that provision. Danny Morris relates a story about a Quaker, John Woolman.

> From 1745 onward, John Woolman spoke out against slavery. He called upon the Friends who were present to free their slaves. There was no consensus, but he was not the only one who felt that leading. Others took the opposite position and could not accept his leading. He went on record in opposition to Friends holding slaves, but the Friends Meeting (their church) counted him in and honored his leading. They said, in effect, "we cannot accept it for ourselves, but we want you to follow your leading. We will do your work, tend your crops, look after your family and provide you income to free you to travel the land and call Friends to free their slaves." They did just that for twenty years while John Woolman went up and down the Atlantic coast doing what God had called him to do. And the Quakers freed their slaves more than a century before the Civil War.[4]

Trust God's power to accomplish God's will and offer it back to us as gift. It may take more than human effort to bring a vision to reality. There is more for which to pray. The final outcome and shape may not yet be visible.

Recognize that some members of the council may have special gifts of "distinguishing among spirits." Their wisdom will be invaluable, modeling a gift that can be cultivated in other members of the group.

While a staff member of the Presbyterian U.S. Board of National Ministries in Atlanta, I enjoyed watching our deliberations. It was a "power board," made up of strong and articulate leaders of the church. But one of the most influential members was an eighty-three-year-old retired history professor, Dr. E. T. Thompson. Dr. Thompson rarely entered into debate, but he did write (constantly). When he raised his hand, everyone quieted down and waited. They knew that Dr. E. T. had been writing and rewriting motions and was now ready to offer his latest version of the mind of the group. Many times a board member would say, "Tell us what we have just decided, Dr. E. T.!" So he did. And so the board came to rely on his discerning ear and eye.

Vision

Here is my vision of a prototype board that earnestly discerns the Spirit:

Every member of this board is daily working at discerning God's will in her own life. Daily prayer and silent listening are on the spiritual menu. Occasional retreats are taken to quiet the inner voices and ego demands. Each member joined the board only after a thorough examination of the invitation to serve as a call from God through the voice of the people.

The board has bonded as a community through the stories they have told and their common experience of the grace of God. They are a diverse group but have grown to hold deep respect for one another and for one another's vocations.

The meetings are conducted in a framework of worship. Members pray openly with and for one another.

Several significant issues or opportunities are before them. They have agreed on the priority matter at hand and are willing to take six months to study, reflect, and pray toward a decision.

The moderator of the group is fair and sensitive—especially to the need to consider each person's wisdom and to look into some connecting biblical passages.

The decisions made are not necessarily the most convenient, cheap, politically palatable, or agreeable to the pastor's wishes. They are agreed upon with one consideration: that God is leading and calling out this particular form of obedience and mission.

In response to the leading, every member prayerfully works for its completion, all the while trusting that God will accomplish more than they ever imagined.

The board maintains a playful spirit, not taking itself too seriously. It is open to celebrate at the drop of a hat what God is doing.

Implementation

The leadership team of the Nashville Academy, an intentional Christian community for prayer and ministry, was stalemated in its effort to sort out a problem related to the daily crowded schedule. The struggle had

gone on for two years, during which team members had become polar-
ized into strongly held positions. Listen to Danny E. Morris's account of
how painlessly the logjam was broken.

> The thing that saved us was the discernment mode to which we were
> committed. At our final meeting we agreed—covenanted—with
> each other to make this issue a matter of earnest prayer during the
> three months before we met again. When the team reassembled, we
> began with a period of silence to center ourselves in the Holy Spirit
> and be present with each other. We called for reports of leadings of
> the Spirit. What followed was almost unbelievable. No one advo-
> cated previously held positions! We discovered that no one had
> talked to another member about the issue. We had prayed about it
> and we had listened, and in less than twelve minutes the matter was
> resolved.[5]

So often boards rush to judgment without consulting and living into
the Spirit. They operate under the illusion that they can push their way
into an efficient use of their decision-making time. The parliamentary
method, being an adversarial process, favors such boards. Those who
speak first, loudest, and most cerebrally carry an inordinate share of
power. Some would even observe that the parliamentary method is a
subtle form of control that limits the common search for a common way.

Robert's Rules of Order may protect us from one another. Yet I
have observed that people use the "Rules" to get their own needs met—
to have fights, display their knowledge, massage their egos, vent their
anger, test their opinions, punish their opponents, cover their fears, and
hide from anything personal.

The parliamentary method assumes that no community base exists
from which to interact and decide. There are appropriate places for its
use—even in church boards. But it is not the foundation on which discernment is built. Prayerful discernment slows down the verbal and
aggressive members, while seeking the wisdom of the silent ones. Prayerful discernment lays aside ego-driven "convictions" and relinquishes
corporate self-will. It seeks to see things whole, through the eyes of
God.

While the Set Apart Lay Leaders model for the integration of
spirituality and administration is not a conflict-resolution model, it does
reduce routine conflict. In the first test year, the five covenant churches

that worked the model showed that positive, open attitudes were eight times more evident than in the five churches that were on their own to integrate spirituality and administration and four times more evident than in the random sampling of churches. Regarding the energy and vitality of meetings, the boards of our covenant churches were much more positive and less negative, making three times more positive references than baseline churches.

There are dangers in reducing discernment to a calculated, step-by-step process. Yet as a board begins its work in discernment, it may need an ordered structure. It's a lot like learning to ride a bicycle.

When I taught my children to ride bikes, I remember instructing them with this step–by–step starting procedure. (1) Point the bike in the direction you want to go. (2) Place the pedal on the opposite side in an "up" position. (3) Put both hands on the handlebars. (4) Swing one leg over the bike and put your foot on the pedal slightly forward from "up." (5) Look ahead, where you want to go. (6) Push!

After a few tries they "got it." It wasn't long before they just jumped on their bikes and rode without any thought to the step-by-step procedure.

So it is with learning to ride the bike called corporate discernment. You may begin with a step-by-step approach. But after a few meetings you find yourselves doing it without procedural calculations. The Presbytery of Cincinnati offers to work with the sessions of their congregations in a step-by-step discernment process they have adapted from an organization in St. Louis. It, as follows, is one example of many that could be used.

Discernment: The Practice of Faithful Listening

The Process

1. Rational stage—Data gathering, sorting out good from bad information and ideas, preparing all information possible.
2. Communication stage—Supplying information to people and educating them so that all understand.
3. Guiding principle stage—What is the issue? What is the result for which we seek guidance?
4. Analytical stage—Eliminate all options which clearly do not relate

to the guiding principle. (Refer good ideas that are not related to other persons or groups so they are not lost.)

5. Intuitive stage:
    a. Allow time for prayerfully considering all information and to prepare a statement about how the guiding principle may be achieved (10–20 minutes, or go home to consider).
    b. Group regathers. Each person reports their statement. (Discussion only, with questions for understanding and clarification. No debate or weaknesses pointed out.)
    c. Ask each person to pray alone, considering each option, looking only for the good in each statement, and asking which has the weightier good.
    d. The group regathers—"List each option and tell your own understanding of the good in each option." (No weaknesses. Add good to good.)
    e. Now each person prays alone, seeking the weightier good. (With the approach and attitude, "I believe in prayer." "I practice prayer." "I am indifferent to which choice God will choose in this issue.")
    f. The group shares each weightier good with the whole group. Test for consensus: "Can you find full support for one weightier good as it emerges?"
        For nonsupporters: "Have all your concerns been heard?" "Can you support the rest?"
        If "no"—ask them to search their hearts for total indifference to which is God's will.
        If indifference is not present—redo the process: "Are principle options right?" "Is the guiding principle right?"
        If after two or three more tests, there is still no consensus, and the group has not heard the will of God and time is out, casting lots [or drawing straws] is better than voting. If a vote is necessary, it is less likely to get divisive. Or depart the scene and seek other options to start over.[6]

This illustration of a working group-discernment model gives us a picture of decisions emerging without a formal vote. It draws the group into active discussion yet in a prayerful way. It engages both the right and left brain, drawing upon the full wisdom of the total group. If you had been a participant, your contribution would have been valued, whether you are of a rational or intuitive bent. Most significant to me, however, is the thought of being engaged in a process that builds on one another's strengths and insights, rather than looking for weaknesses in the positions of others.

CHAPTER 6

Going Somewhere: The Practice of "Visioning" the Future

A Story: Grace United Church Peeks into a Future

Grace Church is the product of a merger between a Methodist church and Presbyterian church in a changing neighborhood. Both churches had been strong in their heydays. But when they merged most of their "hey" was gone, and now the new, united congregation is attempting to minister to and with the new poor and multiracial population of the neighborhood. The constituents of the church include a few old-line members and a mixture of new neighborhood residents drawn to the church through its many neighborhood ministries—food pantry, clothing store, Hispanic outreach, and a variety of programs for children and youth. In addition to the pastor, the staff includes a national missionary, a Hispanic minister, and some part-time specialty workers. Although the church has very little money, it generously stretches what it does have to sponsor a number of visiting youth groups that come to stay in the church and work in the neighborhood. The entire setup reminds one of a new sprout growing from the seed of a collapsing pumpkin, with the old, decaying shell offering nourishment for the tender young plant.

The new council that was formed after the merger was comprised mainly of newcomers. Few council members came to the church with any previous board experience; membership on a church council felt foreign to most. The council, after spending a year in a learning covenant with the Set Apart Lay Leaders project, scheduled a day-long retreat to "vision" their future. I asked them to sit in a circle (as if it were a clock)—in the order in which they came to be associated with the church. Then they personally introduced themselves by telling how they came to be associated with the church, who at the church had influenced them, and how God was opening new doors. The introductions were translated into Spanish for one new council member.

This group would not have been able to come up with a detailed three-year plan. Even now they hardly know what the next year will look like. But they do have a vision they can picture.

Their vision is to be open to God's future, with a commitment to being a celebrative church in the community that cares about its neighborhood. In reviewing their stories, we saw that few of the church's exciting ministries had originated on a planning chart. Programs emerged when something was dumped in the congregation's lap or when a person with special gifts happened in on them. What was already happening had a life of its own and seemed more like a miraculous work of God than an action plan.

Grace Church is appropriately named, for it is open to the gifts that God brings. And God is bringing rich gifts in the form of youth groups that come to work in the neighborhood, a missionary sent by the denomination, several who can communicate and work with Spanish-speaking people—the list goes on. Vision for Grace is commitment to a direction, with adjustments and midcourse corrections dictated by the opportunities and resources that God provides.

Council members like to use the image of people being "hooked" by the church's neighborhood ministries, then being "reeled in" to participate in worship and lay leadership. The council members are enthusiastic about their church.

But efforts to organize them into standard-brand church committees in what I would call a "theological oughtness" model (that is, "we ought to do worship, evangelism, education, and ministry") have frustrated them. They could never get the committees off the ground because they did not seem to "mesh" with the existing patterns of ministry and the constantly forming natural groupings in the church.

At their planning retreat, the council saw a vision for a new possibility. Each group—whether youth or Hispanic or the pantry ministry—could incorporate worship, nurture, evangelism, and ministry into its own being. Leaders could be prepared to work at all of those levels. The council would then serve as a connecting place for all of the natural groups, where information could be exchanged, support rendered, and accountability measured. They would not need an evangelism committee, for instance, because every group would be doing evangelism on behalf of the church.

In the Sunday worship celebration, all of these groups would come together. Each would bring its witness, thanksgivings, and prayer requests. They would sit together under the Word of God.

This vision seemed to fit them, for it was open enough to be responsive to whatever God and people brought. Yet it was specific enough in leadership development, accountability, and patterns of gathering for them to picture it in their minds.

They went home with a vision that was tuned to reality, yet one that would stretch them.

A Master Story: Eldad and Medad Pull a Surprise
Numbers 11:24-29

Moses was described as one who "knew God face to face." God came to Moses as Yahweh, a personal god who enters into relationship with people. And the people Moses led knew of that special relationship. When Moses had been on the mountain or in the tent talking to God, his face had a certain glow that people recognized.

But now God, preparing to enlarge the leadership circle, asked Moses to select seventy elders who would share the burden of leadership. "I will take some of the spirit that is on you and put it on them," declared Yahweh (v. 17). Everything went according to plan:

> So Moses went out and told the people the words of the Lord; and he gathered seventy elders of the people, and placed them all around the tent. Then the Lord came down in the cloud and spoke to him, and took some of the spirit that was on him and put it on the seventy elders; and when the spirit rested upon them, they prophesied (vv. 24-25).

But the story doesn't end there. As in so many stories of Moses, the plot has a twist:

> Two men remained in the camp, one named Eldad, and the other named Medad, and the spirit rested on them; they were among those registered, but they had not gone out to the tent, and so they prophesied in the camp. And a young man ran and told Moses, "Eldad and Medad are prophesying in the camp." And Joshua . . . the

assistant of Moses . . . said, "My lord Moses, stop them!" But
Moses said to him, "Are you jealous for my sake? Would that all
the Lord's people were prophets, and that the Lord would put his
spirit on them!" (vv. 26-29).

Reflective Story Weaving

Eldad and Medad could have fit right in with the council of Grace
Church. They were not very traditional, and, for whatever reason, they
were not associating with religious meetings and places. Instead of
meeting with the elders around the tabernacle, they were in the camp,
where the people were. Grace Church council members would more
likely be found there too—in the neighborhood, involved with people.

Yet Elders Eldad and Medad had the spirit of the Lord and spoke out
of that connection. They prophesied in the camp. The pastor of Grace
Church often remarked to me that she was "amazed" at the simple but
profound spiritual insights that seemed to come out of the council members from time to time. She wondered where that wisdom came from.

A traditional board organization as suggested by the judicatories for
Grace Church does not seem to fit. The structure may serve the judica-
tory and its reporting needs but not the emerging indigenous church.
These people seem more at home in the camp than in the tent.

Leadership is shared downward in both stories as the organizational
pyramid flattens. The new lay leaders emerge seemingly without a lot of
manipulation. When they appear, they are recognized and put to work.

What might Eldad and Medad be saying as they prophesy? No
doubt they would be telling the story of the great exodus deliverance and
reminding the people of the greatness and power of a God who had
rescued them. They would hold forth the vision of a land flowing with
milk and honey, which was to be theirs by the promise of God if only
they would claim it. These two elders would be fulfilling the honorable
office of encouragers. Eldad and Medad would call people to worship
and serve Yahweh instead of the Egyptian gods and call the community
to care for one another.

In distilling wisdom from these stories, we see that: (1) God pushes
at the boundaries and limits we set. (2) Leadership for a faith community
is to hold the Spirit of God central to all that is planned, done, and said.
(3) Leadership is to be shared. (4) God's Spirit is not limited to clergy

nor to church buildings and church meetings. (5) God desires that all
would speak out of a connection with the Spirit.

Discernment

I recently saw a slide presentation detailing the restoration process of the
old observatory on the campus of Park College. Not being an astrono-
mer, I had not fully appreciated how important ideal viewing platforms,
their surrounding environment, the quality of the lenses, and the preci-
sion of their arrangement are in achieving an optimal view of the heavens.

The current desire to understand the nature of leadership and leadership development in American politics and in the society at large always
settles on "the vision thing." You either have it, or you get it, or you
don't!

Not surprisingly, a major theme in trustee leadership for churches
and other not-for-profit organizations is that of vision. Organizations
with leaders who have the capacity to look to and plan for the future are
most likely to endure and succeed.

Observatory Image

Let both the retreat setting and the board table be seen as arenas for
"visioning." Both are structures comparable to the observatories of
astronomers who want to look into the distance.

The foundation for our observatory is the images that come from
the reading and study of scripture. Those foundation stones are (1) the
images of God presented in the scripture and (2) the images of the people
of God as a community of faith. Without this foundation, any attempt at
"visioning" will only produce pipe dreams or ego-driven fantasies.

The building materials for the observatory are an awareness of the
community's particular history and an identity that flows from that history. Every congregation has its own unique story, beginning with the
founding stories and enriched by layers of events, moments, anecdotes,
and spiritual wisdom figures. When those stories are told and retold, the
church or board is re-membered! Every church has an identity, with its
own personality and flavor. Without that clear identity in mind, a board
cannot look to a future.

The viewing platform for our observatory is built out of the values and beliefs held by the faith community. An important prerequisite for looking at the future is identifying current values, beliefs, and basic purpose. Extended retreats can provide a setting in which those can be located and named. Interweaving our stories with the master stories of scripture will reveal important patterns of core values.

The isolated and protected viewing room of the observatory is created out of solitude, silence, prayer, and worship. Observatories need to be located away from noise, vibrations, lights, and pollution. The narrow slit that opens in a retractable roof allows only a limited view, shutting out the whole world of stars and competing lights. If our attempts to look at the future are hurried, cluttered, and activity filled, we will not be able to see past the cumber and din of our current activities. Boards need to develop disciplines of corporate silence, listening, and relinquishment that free them to see.

The telescope equates with our capacity to dream, imagine, and picture a preferred future. It's a picture we need to see as clearly as possible. Boards need to be able to come to a common view to plan for the future that is—or could be—before them.

Allow me to mix metaphors for a few illustrative paragraphs. Picture a large writing board with the outlines of two houses sketched on it, one labeled "is" and the other labeled "will be." On the "is" house write the names of programs, ministries, and activities of the present church that embody values and faith beliefs important to the church. These values may already have been identified and isolated through a process of biblical-theological reflection. Mark the ministries and programs that incorporate those values with a plus sign. Mark those that do not incorporate the values with a minus sign. Carry those with a plus sign over to the "will be" house. Activities with a "minus" sign should be carried over to the "will be" house only if someone can suggest how to convert the minus to a plus.

Participants in the process may see activities "of value" in other churches or in the history and tradition of their own church that they would like to include in their "will be" picture. They can borrow these! Research shows that new ministries are most likely to succeed when people are aware of specific models that are working.

Creativity is not always the fabrication of something brand new; it is more often a new combination of existing things.

Be sure to leave much open space in the new house for the activity of the Spirit. One danger of our highly refined "strategic plans" is that they become efforts to prove our own worth and value. But we do not create the future. The future comes as a gift from God. We are free to "dream dreams and see visions"; that comes with the promise of the Spirit's presence. So draw the blueprint, build the house. But expect the Spirit to change the floor plan, bring in something new, rearrange the furniture, or even throw some things out!

The focusing mechanism in our astronomers' observatory is that meeting-to-meeting effort continually to revisit the new picture and test to see where present activities cloud or blur the image.

UCLA basketball followers used to hear about a "Wooden." It was a picture in the mind of Coach Wooden about how a basketball play was to be run. The picture was so clear to him that any deviation from it in a game or practice demanded adjustment and correction. His players soon caught on as this master coach was able to re-create the picture in their minds. Those years of national championships are attributable to many a "Wooden."

Every board meeting can be compared to a practice court where distortions of the vision are corrected or to an observatory in which the lens is always being adjusted. Objects may shift from the foreground to the background of the picture or vice versa. Noting these shifts, making adjustments, and keeping a value-formulated vision before the church are keys to the exercise of spiritual leadership.

There is one more factor to consider.

The eye, heart, and mind of the viewers internalize the picture seen in the observatory. The viewers go away as changed people. The picture is now a part of their being. They're newly aware that they're connected—that they live in the heavens among the stars. The wonder and mystery of this connection may not be explained, but it is real.

Connections

All four of the practices in the worshipful work model are tied together. They do not operate in isolation. Let's look at the ways they are connected.

Vision is connected to history and stories. We have seen the result of a group being bathed in history and showered by stories. They create an identity within the faith family and a solidarity with the saints and heroes of the ages. People with a clear sense of identity know where they have come from and how certain tunes and melodies play on in them. I have a theory that people become their names. Think of the power of baptism, where the name is blessed and an age-old rite connects the child to parents, the church, Jesus, and John the Baptist. When my children were navigating some rough waters of adolescence or early adulthood, I would remind them that they had been baptized!

History and story create community, the gift of God's grace. That is why re-membering uses stories to re-engraft members into the family. Vision may be a private exercise, but the role of good leadership is to help the community come to a shared vision. A vision that energizes, excites, clarifies, and invites others into it can only emerge from a community base.

History and its lessons will also impose a "reality check" on the vision to see whether or not it is being projected within the values and basic purpose of God's people.

Vision is connected to biblical-theological reflection. The Bible presents a creator God who is the Lord of history. Its opening pages reveal a story of creation, where God brought something to be out of nothing. "What is matter," asked one philosopher, "but a thought in the mind of God?" God must have had a picture of creation that God worked or allowed to work. Creation itself is a picture in the mind of God.

God's encounter with Abraham reveals another picture in the mind of God, a picture that led to a covenant promise. "I will be your God and you will be my people." "You will multiply and become a great nation." In the covenant renewal at Sinai, the picture enlarges until the people become a "nation of priests." Later, God's covenant with David pictures a royal succession culminating in a king who will reign forever.

The *shalom* of God became background for the visions of the prophets. Injustice, war, cheating, or oppression of the poor and helpless was so out of place in the picture that the prophets had no recourse but to confront the established powers and rail against what they saw.

Jesus held forth a picture of the kingdom of God and told stories that illustrated it. Each story was in itself a vision. Where there is no vision, the people perish. Jesus supplied the vision.

Paul continues the thread when he affirms that the new testament community is a foreshadow of the big picture to come. The church is a sign of the kingdom, where all are reconciled in Christ—male and female, Jew and Gentile, slave and free. They are the new community. God's big plan is to unite everything in Jesus Christ—things on earth and things in heaven. If that is our current visual background, then we already have a start in the creation of our visions. If our visions are out of place in that big picture, God will raise up prophets to confront and rail against us as well.

The last book in the Bible is rich with images. A New Jerusalem will come down to earth. God's dwelling will be with a tearless people. There will be a new heaven and a new earth!

Is there any doubt that our capacity to dream and envision is rooted in this story? Furthermore, special sight is given as a gift to the people of God. This is especially true for oppressed people, who have only a vision to hold onto. That vision gives them a special spirit. Note the heavenly images the African slaves in America held in their imprisonment and the "soul" and "spirit" they generated. Their psychic and emotional survival was provided by the visions. God would have the last word.

Vision is connected to discernment. Vision is the gift of divine eyes for seeing the future as it could be. Discernment is the gift of seeing things as they are in the here and now. Values that emerge from theological reflection are carried into a discernment process in the current setting. The issue in discernment becomes "What is God's will and call?"

Vision will focus the same eyes and ears of the Spirit to a future time and setting. The same values of discernment located in a process of theological reflection can be projected into a future setting. What values will be life- and growth-enhancing?

Once a decision or response to God's will, call, and vision has been made, then another story is created. That story, in turn, is laid alongside another master story and the process continues. We have a continuing cycle of spiraling experiences, reflections, discernment, and vision that create an exciting journey of faith!

Vision

My vision is that the Pentecost prophecy would be fulfilled:

> I will pour out my Spirit on all flesh;
> and your sons and your daughters shall prophesy,
> your old men shall dream dreams,
> and your young men shall see visions (Joel 2:28).

This picture could fit the church board!

Identifying and holding forth a vision is an important function of lay as well as clergy leadership. But there is one more step that must be taken.

Unless the vision is worn or embodied by the vision holder, it will have no substance. No one will follow. This is where I challenge boards and councils. If you hold a vision for faithful stewardship in the congregation, it must first be modeled in the board. If you hold a vision for productive evangelism in the church, it will begin with board members who can witness, reflect, and invite. If you hold a vision for a prayerful flock, board meetings must be prayerful. The best place to affect change in the church is in the board. Don't expect anything to happen that doesn't start there! Wear the vision. Embody it together as a board.

Implementation

A strategic plan cannot be equated with a vision, although it may be the product of visionary people. Sometimes our best laid plans are exactly that: our own plans. Parker Palmer suggests that sometimes our planning may be another form of "works" righteousness or an attempt to earn our salvation.[1] If we are good enough and smart enough and powerful enough, the thinking goes, we can lay out the plans and then prove our worth by accomplishing them!

Once we have gone to scripture to catch a glimpse of the image of God and the character of the people of God, we can move toward the preferred picture or vision—all the time remembering that God is going to create the future, not we. God will offer it to us as a gift. So in the meantime, we must be open to midcourse corrections and to special gifts, opportunities, and people who come into the picture, until the vision takes to itself a life of its own.

Once the dis-ease of board lethargy has been named, a preferred vision for a board has been identified as worshipful work, and a construct of our four practices is understood, how should pastors and lay leaders who hold visions for a new way of doing board introduce it? I suggest two approaches.

Rational Presentation

The first is a full, frontal, rational presentation with covenant to test and experience it. The pastor of Trinity Lutheran Church in Shawnee Mission, Kansas, read one of my published articles. He had been yearning for something more for his council. He asked me for an appointment, and then he asked me to meet with his staff and a few key lay leaders. They wanted to understand the model. We arranged for a day-long retreat at which the model could be presented to and experienced by the whole council. Supportive materials were distributed. Following the retreat, the pastoral staff and the council president met monthly with me as consultant to frame the agenda for the next meeting. We reviewed the last meeting and identified what was coming to the next one. We organized an agenda that incorporated some aspect of each of the four practices of the model.

When I hear of the transformational attempts of creative boards, I ask them to send me copies of their agenda. Standard-brand agenda are dreary. But I would like to sit in on some of the more creative ones. That does not mean they are complicated. It does mean that they see what they are doing in the context of worship. Then their decisions are lifted as a holy offering.

A Sneak-It-In Approach

The second approach is to sneak in changes. The administrative board of Trinity United Methodist Church in Kansas City, Kansas, already had a full plate with staffing decisions and a change in ministry directions. The pastor and board president had a commitment and vision to do board better. They were responsible for setting the agenda.

They followed some advice similar to what I heard Don Griggs give to a group of ministers and educators at our Heartland retreat center.

After Don led a workshop—The Use of the Bible in Committee Meetings—a participant asked for advice on a strategy for introducing this back home. Don replied, "Don't go back and present it as some new, dramatic program and ask them to vote on it. Just begin doing it because you are the people of God and that is what God's people do! After a while they will think they have always done it this way!"

PART 3

An Open Letter to Board and Council Members

(With Permission Granted for Pastors, Council Moderators, and Church Nominating Committees to Read)

CHAPTER 7

Fathoming the River: To Those Considering a Call to Service

Faced with a Decision

Your phone rings. The person on the other end of the line tells you that he/she represents your church's nominating committee, which is seeking nominees for the official board. He/she invites you to meet together to discuss your openness to serving the church as one of its "set apart" lay leaders—as an elder, deacon, council or vestry member. You are willing to hear the presentation. You agree to the meeting. You also agree to make it a matter of prayer and personal reflection.

As you place the receiver back in its cradle, your mind races ahead. Who, me? Why me? Am I worthy? You may have hoped and prayed for (or perhaps dreaded) this call for years. Suddenly the time is at hand. What will you decide?

It's as if you are standing beside an ever flowing stream. That stream represents lay leadership which has served, is serving and will serve the church in a set apart capacity through a church board or council. I want to explore with you what you need to know and consider before you join the crew—to fathom the stream you have been invited to travel and the nature of the boat you are about to board for the trip downstream.

I want to discuss with you the nature of a "call," the meaning of spiritual leadership, the character of church boards and councils, the unique gifts which you can bring, and what you can expect in the experience. I want to introduce you to one of the very high privileges in the church—serving on a church board. Some may not consider it so attractive, but I enthusiastically choose to hold it before you in that light.

Let me tell you two stories. The first is told by Don Goeller, Council Chairman of All Saints Parish in St. Peters, Missouri:

A Story: From the Cradle to the Council

I was a cradle Catholic, raised in the church. But I drifted away from the church while I was in the Army. I went back after my Army days, but my faith was routine, involving me in liturgy, lector reading, and music. Although I had volunteered for a lot of things in the parish, the first time I ever considered a "call" was upon the invitation to serve as a member of the parish council. Since I was relatively new to the parish I figured that the call must have come from God, for I had not earned my way into the center of parish leadership.

The invitation to serve on the parish council really began a faith journey for me. I began to express my faith—to listen to and open up to people. The council's manners invited and encouraged me to do that. This led me to a greater challenge—to involvement in the wider community.

The council went through the normal stages of group development with its intellectual aspects but soon moved to a spiritual focus because we members felt a hunger for it and Fr. Henning held a vision for it. So when we found ourselves getting mechanical, focusing only on policies, we had to reexamine ourselves to keep a God centered focus. We were challenged to keep a spiritual edge. Whether we were working on a stewardship effort or a smoking policy related to Bingo (which was a really big issue!), we found that we needed to work toward consensus. The only way to really do that was from a spiritual base which was rooted in our sense of call.

A Master Story: From "But" to "Yes"

The second story comes from our biblical tradition. Moses' account of his call (based on Exodus 2-4) could have sounded something like this:

I had just gone through a very difficult time in my life. Back in Egypt, life in Pharaoh's court had lost its glitter and I increasingly longed to know more of my own heritage. But there was one problem. My people were slaves! I hadn't realized how much I was one of them until the day I beat to death the Egyptian oppressor of one of my brother Israelites.

I fled for my life because Pharaoh was after me. Adjusting to the life of a desert nomad was tough; a shepherd's meal of goat cheese and coarse bread was a far cry from Pharaoh's banquet table. There was some consolation during those fear-ridden days. I met and married the daughter of a desert priest and began to raise a family. Jethro, my new father-in-law, was kind to me and accepted me into his family. He was a very special person—not only kind, but full of special wisdom born of the desert. We used to sit around the campfire in the evenings for hours on end, speaking of the things of God.

One day while I was tending Jethro's sheep near the mountain of God, a strange sight drew my attention. A bush seemed to be burning but was not consumed! On approaching it for a closer look, I thought I heard someone call my name. At first I thought I was hearing things. But the voice persisted, and I took it to be the voice of God. Then the voice confirmed that it was the voice of the God of my mothers and fathers and of my people. I was scared to death, but did have the presence of mind to take off my shoes, for this was surely holy ground.

I had some limited awareness of the import of that eventful visit—that God wanted me to return to Egypt and bring my people out to a land of promise. But in the ensuing days I kept going back there in my mind to wrestle with what it meant and whether I would be willing to say "yes." Jethro, my wife Zipporah, and I talked about it day in and day out. We concluded that this was in fact "Yahweh" speaking, a God who enters into personal relationship and goes with his people—and that this God had a special task for me to do. God had indeed heard the groaning prayers of the people in Egypt and was going to do something about their plight . . . beginning with me!

But how I fought it! I had five good reasons to say "no" to Yahweh. Every one of them began with a "but." (1) But who am I to go? It would be presumptuous for me. (2) But I don't even know your name! (3) But they won't believe you have appeared to me and will not listen to me. (4) But I am not an eloquent speaker, not even since we met. (5) But please send someone else.

Yahweh was very patient with me. Jethro's counsel was helpful as well. Every one of my "buts" had a response. God gave me his name and a promise. God provided some tangible signs and gifts which the people would acknowledge. God reminded me that God even created my tongue (but God fudged on that one by appointing my brother Aaron my spokesman).

So I decided to say "yes" and prepared to go back to Egypt. Jethro gave me his blessing and agreed to take care of Zipporah and the kids. So I was off to Egypt!

Distilling Wisdom

I would like to invite you to take some time to add your own story to those of Don and Moses. Write it out—from the initial approach to your making your decision. Then do some story weaving. Compare notes with Don and Moses. What do you share in common? What is unique and distinct for you? At the end of the story weaving, draw some conclusions from your experiences. Distill the common wisdom.

Without knowing your story, I would venture to predict some of the wisdom statements you'll discover in the two I've related to you. (1) The calls were not sought. They were initiated by God or from elsewhere. Other people were involved in the instigation or reflections upon the call. (2) An element of "mystery" accompanied the calls. Circumstances of timing and placement announced, "There is more going on here than initially meets the eye." (3) God's presence can be found in and around the call. God came with a willingness to enter into a personal relationship and "be with" the called person through it all. (4) Calls can be couched in the ethos of human pain or in a vision that things can be different. Calls come from heaven but are very earthy. (5) Calls were validated by people in the faith community, either in initiation or by blessing. (6) Human feelings can be triggered by a call and need to be faced and processed; whether positive or negative, initial feelings do not finally determine the validity of a call from God

You can add or subtract from this list after weaving your story with the others.

Assessing the element of "call" in your invitation to serve will be crucial to your effectiveness on the board. An article published by The Alban Institute observes, "If groups are formed out of a sense of vocation rather than merely volunteerism, the people's service is seen as connected closely to their spiritual journey, the burnout factor decreases and the value of the service to people's lives increases."[1]

Assessing your call will be an intensely personal experience for you —one that takes you to the core of your identity as a person, to your spiritual journey of faith, and into a dynamic encounter with the living God.

So look for God's presence in the call. But know that your call will arise out of the community of faith as they recognize their needs, your gifts, and God's calling. The community both initiates and validates the call.

Consider the instance of Elijah casting his mantle over Elisha. God used the very human decisions of Elijah in the selection of Elisha. When plowing a field, Elisha was faced with a decision. To signal his affirmative response, he sacrificially offered a team of oxen to God rather than giving them to Elijah, his mentor. The offering was roasted on a fire made with the oxen's wooden yoke. Then the community (neighbors) ate the roasted offering in a feast, symbolically validating the call from God!

The church's nominating committee may be your "Elijah." Prayers of relinquishment and discernment may robe your "yes." The congregation's participation in your ordination or installation ritual compares to the validating feast—setting you apart for leadership with their blessing.

A Look Downstream for Tradition

In approaching this stream called spiritual leadership, you will need to fathom the nature of it—its depth, width, direction, and rate of flow, as well as its eddies, its hazards, and its beauty. You will also want to look downstream to see what has passed by in the way of tradition.

Elders in Israel

You're in good company as you consider the call to serve a community as one of its spiritual leaders. No matter what portion of the historic waters we look at downstream, "elders" will appear.

G. K. Chesterton said that tradition is the only true democracy because it means giving a vote to your ancestors![2] Our spiritual ancestors are the men and women out of the pages of biblical history. The Hebrew wisdom literature refers to elders as the wise and assigns them a very special role. Since obedience to God was required, opportunities for obtaining counsel were essential. Three classes of experts functioned within Judaism to provide this needed counsel. (1) *The prophets* addressed the political and moral issues of the nation. (2) *The priests* conducted worship and cultic rites. (3) *The wise (hakhamim)* counseled people about the good life and proper conduct (Jer. 18:18).

The elders were the wise and widely respected natural leaders of their communities. The word *elder* originally meant "with full beard" or "an old man," but it soon came to be associated with wisdom, godliness, and honor. There are 125 references to elders in the Hebrew scriptures, indicating the vital role they played in Israel's life.

In the New Testament period, we see elders within the powerful ruling body of "the seventy." The Sanhedrin consisted of three classes of members: (1) priests, (2) scribes, who represented the strictly orthodox Pharisees, and (3) elders, lay members from respected and influential families. The elders provided the much needed practical and political wisdom that balanced the assembly.

When we look to the Jewish synagogues of Jesus' day, we see a special role for elders. They did not have responsibility for worship. Neither were elders administrative officials. Rather, they were natural, trusted leaders who functioned as counselors.

Elders in the Christian Church

Four Greek words describe "set apart" leaders in the New Testament.

Presbuteros (elders) were the spiritually mature and morally upright. They functioned in plurality, as a group. Their commitment to Christ, evidence of the power of the Holy Spirit, was held in common, even though their gifts and tasks may have been diverse. *Character* was their hallmark.

Diakonoi (deacons) were the servants, attendants, associates, or deputies for ministry. Their qualifications were nearly the same as those of elders. Deacons were appointed (Acts 6) to lighten the load of table service for the apostles.

Episcopos (overseers) were responsible officers whose important functions were to supervise, watch, and guard.

Paimen (pastors) were those who gave special care to the people. Their hallmark was *attitude*.

These four designations are not distinct offices in the church, although historically some have tried to find a biblical governing pattern in them. New Testament writers sometimes used the words interchangeably in reference to a particular person.

The pastoral epistles provide us with a picture of "set apart" leaders (1 Tim. 3 and Titus 1) in behavioral images that stand in contrast to Roman culture. An elder's character is to be: above reproach; committed to one wife; self controlled; sensible and prudent; respectable; hospitable; teaching, exhorting and refuting; free from addiction to wine; peaceable; gentle; even tempered; free from love for money; good managers of the household; generous stewards; loving, limit-setting parents; of good reputation outside the church; fair; zealous for the good; devout.

Lay Leaders in History

As the church closed the second century, its leadership patterns became more varied. Some took on a hierarchical structure, with the overseeing (bishop) function concentrated in one person. This concentration continued to develop until the Reformation ushered in alternative patterns of order in church life. The Swiss reformers concluded that clergy and laity were equal, and that leadership for the local church should be shared by a group of elders. The elders would bear rule in the church and exercise discipline. In German Lutheran circles, the authority for the pastor would be found in preaching the Word of God and administering the sacraments.

John Calvin was uncomfortable with a hierarchical form of governance; at the same time he could not tolerate the potential chaos of every person living unto the self. Calvin resorted to a well-defined constitution for the church around Paul's mandate to do things "decently and in order." He cited the priesthood of all believers (1 Peter), assuming that leaders would surface from the faith community to share authority. Pastors and teachers would preach and teach. Deacons would care for the poor. The elders would govern and "correct faults." The elders would possess gifts of the Spirit. They would lead under the prompting of the Holy Spirit.

The composite picture of boatloads of "set apart" leaders navigating history's river has clarity, color, variety, and sharpness that transcend culture and time. You now consider boarding a boat in that stream. Your issues are not unlike those of biblical or historic saints of the church. Are you ready to place yourself "in the same boat" as a spiritual leader?

The people who have invited you to lead through membership on the church board have a difficult and noble task. Increasingly, I see these nominating or discernment groups approach their work in a careful and prayerful manner. Their work can be made difficult, especially if people rotating off the board are vocally negative about their experience. This book attempts to change that by helping churches to transform boards into life-giving bodies.

You may want to compare your experience of being approached by a nominating group with the experience of more than six hundred church board members surveyed: [3]

	Agree	Agree/Disagree	Disagree
I was encouraged to consider the request prayerfully	61%	18%	20%
The committee gave me a clear explanation of the meaning of the office	50%	26%	24%
The committee gave me a clear explanation of the of the duties of the office	49%	23%	29%
I was confronted with the importance of responding to God's call	48%	25%	26%
The committee appeared to be simply trying to fill empty slots	20%	19%	61%

	Agree	Agree/Disagree	Disagree
The committee wanted me to respond immediately to their request	19%	19%	62%
The committee trivialized the importance of the office	6%	9%	85%

While prayer and consideration of God's call are generally included and important, you can see that there is much room for growth.

Committees would do well to consider the pattern Jesus followed in preparation for choosing the twelve disciples. "[Jesus] went out to the mountain to pray" (Luke 6:12a). The Lord removed himself from distractions and secular influences on his choices. He persisted for a good length of time: "and he spent the night in prayer to God" (v. 12b). The selections did not come easily out of natural affinity, friendship patterns, or out of prevailing cultural standards such as wealth, position, power, education, or synagogue standing. In announcing the chosen twelve, Jesus set them apart with a new name: "And when day came, he called his disciples [a large group] and chose twelve of them, whom he also named apostles" (v. 13).

Your Expectations

Back to your story as a prospective board member. Before making your final decision about embarking on this journey, you would do well to look ahead—to look up stream in anticipation of what might come. What are your deeply held expectations and hopes for yourself and the council if you enter the boat? Again, you may want to compare your expectations with those identified by the six hundred board members in our test group: [4]

	Yes	No
Opportunity to serve the church	100%	0%
Feeling of doing something meaningful	98%	2%

	Yes	No
Fellowship with other elders	95%	5%
Sense of fulfillment	93%	7%
Opportunity to solve problems	93%	7%
Growth in my faith	92%	8%
Opportunity to support the pastor	91%	9%
Work closely with the pastor	86%	14%
Efficient meetings	83%	17%
Opportunity to resolve conflicts	75%	25%
Opportunity to share in prayer	72%	28%

Your Decision

How will you go about making your decision? The decision cannot be taken lightly. It calls for a time of prayer and serious reflection. Rather than going it alone, you may want to take a spiritual friend or trusted small group into your confidence. I remember seeing two parishioners frequently having breakfast together in a local restaurant. They met there weekly to be accountable to each other for the "callings" they were working or considering.

I know the temptation can be powerful to back away because of self-doubt or unworthiness. Yes, in fact, you are unworthy. We all are! Yet God puts his treasure in "common clay pots." His strength is made perfect in our weakness. God chose to free the weakest and poorest people on earth (slaves in Egypt) and make of them a mighty people (Israel) who would do great things—but all the credit would belong to God. Perhaps God wants to do a mighty work in your church through you, rather than by your own ingenuity or effort. When that happens, God alone can be praised.

As you pray remember that those who are inviting you to leadership have been praying as well; they have seen something in you that makes them willing to trust you with the life of the church. They have identified you as a trustee, not just of the financial affairs of the church, but also—and more important—of its spiritual welfare.

Here are some helpful suggestions that you might consider in making your decision.

Focus on God's power, love, and will. Since this may be a call from God, take time to pay attention. Recall all the names for God and Jesus Christ. Finish a series of sentences that begin "You are . . ." and "I praise you for. . ." A good hitter keeps an eye on the ball, following its speed and spin. Pay close attention to the ways and character of God. Make your decision in this light.

Become familiar with the scriptural traditions about leadership. Immerse yourself in several stories about some of the Hebrew and Christian heroes of the faith. See what odds they overcame as they remained faithful to the heavenly call.

Look to your own desires. Your desire to serve on a board in the church may be intense. That's okay. Don't shy away from that. Some think that if they want something, they shouldn't have it—or that it must be a selfish streak that may offend God. God may even love us enough to let our desires shape the call!

Yet, we know that not all our desires are of God. Rest assured that this perplexing issue is not a new one that you alone face. When Paul wrote to Timothy, he made legitimate the place of human desire in office seeking. "The saying is sure: whoever aspires to the office of bishop [overseer] desires a noble task" (1 Tim. 3:1). God uses our desires in the call process. The call doesn't have to taste and smell like nasty medicine. It can have the enticing aroma of a delicious meal.

Consider whether you have some destiny to fulfill. A number of people have "always known" or have had some deep-down hunch that they were meant to do or be something.

My friend Tom Barton has engaged in a number of vocations—teacher, coach, administrator, consultant, youth minister, and computer programmer. But deep down he feels that his "life work" is to research, write, and teach on the subject the Bible in the Arts. The tug won't go away. The shape and form of the work is yet unclear. But the pull persists—especially when the waters of his life become still and he reflects beside that pool of clear discernment.

If you have seen yourself as a church leader, now may be the time to act on the dream. Perhaps a vision lies deep within you that may be discovered out of the quiet depths.

Elijah did not discover God in the wind or fire or earthquake but in the "still small voice." Out of the stillness he realized he was not alone. He recovered a vision for Israel and the world. He then rose to take specific actions in response to that call, fulfilling his destiny.

Check your motivation. Peter, for instance, gives advice to his fellow elders. Consider these four points: (1)"Tend the flock . . . exercising the oversight. (2) not under compulsion but willingly . . . (3) not for sordid gain but eagerly. (4) do not lord it over . . . but be examples" (1 Pet. 5:2–3).

You don't have to say "yes" to the invitation in front of you. But if you do, your willingness to serve will come as a response to the love and grace of God. God was emptied, taking the form of a servant and coming to live and die for humanity—friends. We should strive to perceive our motivation in this light!

If you are truly obedient to God's will, there will be no "shameful gain." That is, you will not accept a board position to elevate yourself into a privileged position. The church leader is not to use people but to serve them.

Neither is there to be "domination over." Our identity is not to be established by exercising control over people. Identity comes from God's gift of love, freeing us from control needs. Examples of serving the flock have been set by none other than the "chief shepherd" (1 Pet. 5:4). Your reward will not be domination but the unfading crown of glory. Sam Fulton, a generous lay steward, used to say, "You can't take it with you, but you can send it on ahead!" He is now enjoying his advanced gifts! Remember: Only God can reward—and God will!

Check with a spiritual friend. The decision is still yours, but thinking out loud and trusting your journey with another (or the two or three gathered) ensures that Christ dwells in your midst. As a pastor, I could always count on several people approaching me in the month of November; they had been approached by the church nominating committee and wanted to think out loud about the spiritual aspects of the invitation.

Know your church's tradition and structure for spiritual leaders. What is the shape of this particular boat? What oars will be placed in your hands? What are the expectations? Do they lie within your values, priorities, and vision of faith? These expectations will form the basis of an eventual covenant. Don's story of his calling at All Saints

Parish put him in touch with God, himself, his rich Catholic tradition, and the important ministries of the parish.

In the final analysis, you may have many good reasons to say "no" or "later." Only you can decide that. But once you have said "yes," your ministry in the church is no longer a matter of convenience or choice. You will have made a covenant with God and the faith community. Be sure to count the cost, for there is a cost to be counted. Many have said that what most surprised them about their board experience was the amount of work to be done.

Once you put your hand to the oar, you can't afford to look back. Jesus taught us about the foolishness of not counting the cost. But the voyage ahead can be glorious. If you enter the boat and launch into the stream, come in faith.

CHAPTER 8

Preparing to Embark:
To Elected Board Members
Preparing for Service

Your decision has been made. If you said "yes," you will need to prepare for the extended journey of a term of office on the board. Most terms are for three years, so good preparation now can enhance your effectiveness and satisfaction in service.

A Story: Mike Loves Mary

Here is a story about Mike, who was both the custodian and a council member in a New Jersey church. His story has been widely told in council leadership circles. The council in Mike's parish was trying to make a transition from the "pay, pray, and obey" syndrome of the pre-Vatican II days to active lay participation on the council. The council had decided to open each meeting by having one council member pick a biblical character and tell how that character influences (1) the council and (2) that individual member's life. Mike protested the idea. He didn't like having to hang around the extra half hour that the meeting extended before closing up the church.

Eventually, it was Mike's turn. Everyone assumed he would pass; they were prepared to move on into the agenda, when Mike stopped them.

Wait a minute, he said. For six months I have been listening to you tell about the biblical character who connects with you. Now you will have to listen to me. All my life I have been a Martha. I have been a Martha to you and to this church for years. Not only that, when I go home I am also a Martha. For twenty-seven years I have been caring for my wife, who is house-bound with crippling arthritis. My late-night return home after closing up the church has been a burden to both of us.

But now that I have heard your stories, I have begun to participate as a Mary. When I go home, I share your stories with my wife. She sent a letter that I want to read to you: "Thank you for giving me back my husband. Mike used to return home too tired to talk, and I had nothing to say. But the past few months he has come home telling stories, reading me the Bible passages that were discussed. Sometimes we even sing! My old beloved Mike is back!"

A Master Story: Sister Acts

Mike just introduced you to Martha and Mary. They, too, have a story to tell. Martha speaks:

Since I am the verbal and more forward sister, I will step forward and tell you about us. Mary and I are very different. I am quick to speak and like to plan and get things done. As a result, I usually end up in the kitchen. I can become resentful of Mary when I need help and she is off in another world. She is less verbal and more artistic. She feels deeply and is very intuitive. When Jesus came for a visit (late, I might add) after our brother's death, I went out to confront him about his tardiness. We ended up in a big theological conversation about the resurrection. I told him that I do believe!

When sister Mary came along a few minutes later, she told him the same thing that I had said, "If you had been here, my brother would not have died." She spoke her words with tears. Instead of getting into a theological discussion, she had even Jesus in tears!

I plan and save but she spends lavishly. If you only knew what that pound of pure perfume cost that she poured over Jesus' feet! She even wiped his feet with her hair. Jesus didn't seem to mind. He was content to allow her to sit in silence at his feet. She was with him at the cross, and also at the tomb, so she was the first to know.

I can say one thing for sure—in spite of the differences between Mary and me, Jesus loved us both the same. There was never any doubt about that.

Weaving Your Story

Add your own story to that of Mike, Mary, and Martha. How are you
like or different from them? Allow your stories to weave together.
When you do, nuggets of refined wisdom will emerge, such as: (1)
Every person is a unique and distinct creation by God. (2) Each person's
gifts have a special place and use in the Christian community. (3) God's
love and grace extend to all people despite their differences.

When you approach service on a board, you bring your unique self.
A four-year-old munchkin in my wife's preschool class gained the attention and admiration of his fellow students and teachers. One day
Johnny bounded from his car, dashed into the church, hung his coat on a
hook, burst into the classroom, placed his hands on his hips, and announced with a strong voice, "Here I am!" He felt good about himself and
was ready to face any new learning adventures that he might encounter.

Some of Johnny's classmates arrived with fear and trepidation.
What will become of me, they seemed to be asking themselves, *if I mix in
with these strangers and try something I've never done before?*

How is it with you? Did we really learn everything we need to
know in kindergarten? These children illustrate how board members feel
when coming for the first time to this new arena of service. Some come
fearfully. Others come with boldness. When one reads the Book of
Acts, a startling impression jumps off the page. These people—from all
walks of life—were bold. They had a good sense of their unique individuality. They were alive in Christ by the power of the Holy Spirit and
had a high calling to fulfill. They enthusiastically shared the good news
and courageously showed it forth in a radical style of living.

You can count on being valued as you prepare to board this vessel.
You should not view your arrival as the addition of just another cog on
the wheel of church machinery. You are not there as a pawn to be manipulated by high-stakes rollers of ecclesiastical bureaucracy. You as a
person are important. You are somebody. God didn't create anyone like
you, nor has life shaped anyone else's experiences exactly like yours.
No other person has been granted your unique gifts. You're about to
become an irreplaceable member of the ship's crew. So stride with
confidence down the pier.

What to Bring on Board

Bring Your Feelings

Bring your feelings on board with you. You couldn't erase the imprint of
powerful feelings that have shaped your life anyway, even if you wanted
to. But you don't want to deny yourself the capacity as a human to enter
this ministry with a full range of human emotions. Count your experience and your capacity to feel emotions (even the so-called negative
ones) as gifts from God. They can be guides to bring you into the fullness of God's love and a means for healing and reconciliation in the
church. When Paul advises the Roman church leaders to "rejoice with
those who rejoice, weep with those who weep" (12:15), he asserts that
the law of Christ is being fulfilled! Boards need all kinds of personality
temperaments, including the highly analytic and deeply empathetic.

Bring Your Needs

Bring your own needs. They can never be checked at the luggage desk.
We are always working to get our needs met, even in board meetings.
Observe a few meetings and you'll see. But needs can be used for the
accomplishment of the divine purpose.

Bring Your Spirituality

When I serve as a spiritual director, I watch for two movements within
the directee: letting go and taking hold. Barry and Connoly summarize
these two dynamics of faith in *The Practice of Spiritual Direction.*

> The "First" dynamic is that stage when the directee is desirous of,
> and struggling against, the Lord's willingness to love him or her and
> save him or her, warts, moles, and all. The great achievement of this
> dynamic is the directee's freedom to receive love, salvation, forgive-
> ness from the Lord. The "Second" dynamic represents the struggle
> of the retreatant to take on the values of Jesus, identify with him,
> and care for what he cares for. The achievement is companionship

with Jesus, the directee's freedom to give or to serve as Jesus gave and served.[1]

You will experience "corporate spirituality" on your board. This is a foreign idea to many because of our orientation to individuality. Together you will be called upon to "let go" and to "take hold." When these have become grace-full practices in your own personal life, you enhance the possibility of their being practiced by your board.

Oswald Sanders differentiates between natural leadership and spiritual leadership.

Natural Leadership	Spiritual Leadership
Self-confident	Confident in God
Knows people	Also knows God
Makes own decisions	Seeks God's will
Ambitious	Self-effacing
Originates own methods	Finds God's methods
Enjoys commanding others	Delights to obey God
Motivated by personal considerations	Motivated by love for God and people
Independent	God dependent[2]

Bring Your Character

Leadership on a board requires more than the individual's natural gifts and traits. As important as these may be, there is one thing more—character. You may think that boards are made up of a bunch of characters, but characters do not necessarily produce character! Character is rooted in faith traditions and values. Character makes people willing to suffer for the values and visions they hold. (Witness the board that takes an unpopular position out of deeply held convictions.) How does character develop? Character develops by attaching yourself to and being true to a story that is bigger than yourself. Great families that produce great leaders have stories and traditions that shape the identity of their children. Nations produce leaders out of their patriotic stories and myths. The church creates leaders whose character is shaped by the story of God's redemptive activity in history through the people of God—Israel and the church. That story has power to transform people and boards. Read on.

In a *materialistic* world full of greed and lust, our story says, "Strive first for the kingdom of God . . . and all these things will be given to you as well" (Matt. 6:33).

In a *seductive* world that asks for our hearts and souls, our story says, "Love the Lord your God with all your heart, and with all your soul, and with all your strength, and with all your mind; and your neighbor as yourself" (Luke 10:27).

In a world that *desires freedom* and liberation ("Don't be dependent on anyone or anything. Become liberated from parents, spouses, and God"), our story says, "Let the same mind be in you that was in Christ Jesus" (Phil. 2:5; subjection to Christ), and, "Be subject to one another out of reverence for Christ" (Eph. 5:21; subjection to the church, the faith community).

In a world where people and nations desperately try to *survive* by arming themselves to the teeth, our story says, "Lose your life. . . . Not my will, but yours be done." When God is out of the picture, survival becomes the ultimate good. When God is in the picture, we can let go. We know there is more to life than our survival.

Prepare Well through Disciplines

Begin your preparation by entering into personal disciplines of scripture reading, prayer, and reflection. If the church is to have leaders who are powerful and alive in the Spirit, full of love and grace, and sensitive to the work and word of God acting in people's lives, those same leaders must be disciplined. The word *discipline* often has harsh and severe overtones. Think of it as meaning simply "practice." Just as an athlete practices a move, swing, shot, stride, or throw until it becomes so natural as to be used without calculation in the heat of a contest, so the spiritual disciplines provide practice in unself-consciously loving and relating to God.

An elder recently approached me with personal insight into a psalm that suggested that the practice of disciplines was like digging channels to the roots of desert plants. The water may not be there yet, but when it arrives, the plant will be ready to receive it!

Call to Scripture

Root yourself in scripture. The Bible shapes the life of the disciple and is used as a source of support and guidance for the spiritual leader. Discipline in scripture study is important for two reasons.

First, God calls upon you to make decisions affecting the life and mission of a faith community; those decisions must be informed by a larger story. If you see your personal story as the continuation of God's story of redemption and release, you live out the master story.

Don't feel that you have to know the whole Bible to be an effective board member. But a willingness to engage in serious study individually and with others will enhance your ministry.

The second rationale for practicing scriptural discipline is more personal. You will need support, encouragement, comfort, and challenge as a leader, and daily scripture reading can provide all four.

Call to Prayer

Prayer is an essential discipline for a council as a whole and for its individual members. Unfortunately, its presence is not always welcomed. I know of one situation in which the board leaders scheduled a prayer time at the beginning of each meeting. Most of the members came into the room when the prayers were over—when the "real meeting" began. One pastor says his board members openly informed him that he was not ever to call the board together for prayer because they would not come.

But Ed Whelan, a pastor who relates with our project, tells an interesting story from a parish he formerly served in Noel, Missouri. This small Episcopal congregation had eighteen members and struggled to stay open until the death of a particular matriarch; with her passing they would feel free to close the church. The matter was being discussed in a vestry meeting when one of the members suggested that they should pray for growth. The other four vestry members scoffingly laughed out loud. Ed stopped them.

"It seems," he said, "that this is one of the most important discussions we have had in this vestry and you laugh at it. Let's take a look at it." Through his skilled and sensitive leadership, they emerged from the meeting with all five members promising to pray daily for growth in the church for the period of a year. One year later when Ed opened a worship service, he saw fifty-two people in front of him; the five vestry members stood across the back of the church with smiles on their faces and tears in their eyes. They had given up their seats to accommodate the crowd!

There are no simple answers to growth dynamics in a church—even prayer. But the point is that when this group agreed in prayer about a matter, it made a difference in the church.

Every board member also needs to cultivate an active and varied practice of prayer. Prayer may take place in three settings. (1) In the great congregation (the sanctuary), the corporate and communal praises, prayers, and offerings are lifted. (2) In the intimate setting of a primary group of people who know one another (the house), shared stories, feelings, and hopes touch God and the group. (3) In solitude and aloneness (the closet), the individual touches the mystery of God's presence. The Holy Spirit prompts from within, bringing one into immediate awareness of God's presence, love, and power. Worship and prayer in the sanctuary, house, and closet form a steady base like a three-legged stool. Take any one leg away and the stool topples.

A solid prayer and worship life emerges from all three settings. Don't focus on the sanctuary and expect it to fulfill the function of the "house." An hour in the wilderness of God's creation is important, but it cannot substitute for singing "A Mighty Fortress Is Our God" with the great congregation. We may commit to prayer with a small group for several hours, discovering how growth-producing this can be. But daily personal prayer is the hardest prayer discipline to maintain. We know we ought to carve out the time; we make repeated, courageous attempts, but we soon find schedules encroaching or we're side-tracked by internal distractions. We may resist passively, not wanting to face the pain inherent in stripping away our attachments, vanity, and egos through the self–denial of the cross. Yet the sweetness of Christ's presence counterbalances the pain as we discover our true selves in him.

Find a rhythm of time and place that works for you. Tune it to your daily work, rest, or meal schedule. Add to that some extended retreats or desert days. The most helpful devotional guide I have come across is *A Guide to Prayer for Ministers and Other Servants*. It proposes one hour per day, one day per month, and one week per year in a private retreat and includes twelve different models for personalizing retreats.[3]

Call to Fast

Jesus often uttered the verb *fast* in the same breath with *pray*. Why?
Jesus knew how we become attached to our ego needs, to things that
measure our worth, to positions that define our value. All of these false
gods lead to death. Fasting is a symbolic process of self-denial—stripping away everything but our dependence on God.

Sometimes career or work becomes central to our sense of being.
Through it we may exert power over others, experience success, and
productively invest our insights and energies. As career becomes an
extension of the self, we defend and protect what we have. We dare not
fail. Eventually career is our god. The same can happen with an avoca-
tion, a project, or even a family. A study on Christian growth says:

> We cannot make any of them the very center of our lives, because
> none of them is God. Each of them ultimately passes away. Each is
> only a part of life, not the Source of life itself. When we center our
> lives on anything but God, we live "according to the flesh." And
> this, whether we know it or not, is living toward death. In life
> "according to the Spirit"—life "in Christ"—our lives and everything
> that gives them value and meaning are not absolutely located in or
> dependent upon what we human beings can do or create or protect.
> Rather, our lives are located "in Christ." God present to us in Jesus
> Christ becomes the source of our energy, the One on whom every
> aspect of our lives depends and to which it is oriented. Life's
> meaning, value, and direction are all funded by and gathered to-
> gether in Jesus Christ.[4]

The discipline of fasting begins with this question: What owns,
controls, or drives you? Naming the influences, accompanied by denial
of food, can become a path of surrender to the love and care of God.

Call to Generosity

In addition to Bible study and prayer, consider the practice of active and
generous stewardship of time and money. Don't expect the stewardship
commitment of the congregation to rise above that of its board.

Those of you who enter into a position of lay leadership should have
developed the graces of hospitality and generosity. You can't ask a

church to stretch and give sacrificially unless you are willing to model the same in your own life. This requires honesty with oneself, for you can't fool God or the community.

I know of one small group in which all members bring copies of their IRS Form 1040 for an open annual review by the group. They lovingly deal with each other and the values reflected in the forms. Our own bent to privacy speaks against this practice. But I wonder how a board might be different if it adopted the practice. I have never seen it done in a board. Are there any takers?

Call to Special Graces

Stewardship involves more than time and money. You may have unique talents and experiences that the church particularly needs at this time. Your call to serve may be a recognition of your gifts. The very exciting "discernment" selection process that a number of Catholic parishes are using seeks to discover, call forth, and affirm each prospective council member's gifts. A group of forty or so really "goes at it," grappling with who among them will finally serve on the parish council.

The Holy Spirit gifts the church with power. One expression of the Spirit can be seen in the gifts God bestows upon the church. These gifts edify and build up the body rather than the individual. The community bonds together by means of the Spirit, even though the gifts may vary. (See appendix 3 on the location of gifts.)

Call to Destiny

In some ways your whole life has been a preparation for putting your gifts to work. The American coach of a U.S. Olympic hockey team told his team before they faced their powerful Russian opponents, "Remember, you were born for this moment."

Here is a test for you to use when attempting to discern God's calling to a particular ministry: Has every major experience and training that I have had to this moment prepared me for this task? Don't discount your experiences, even if they have occurred in nonreligious or non-church settings. Those too may be very valuable. Don't discount the painful experiences and failures. They may have been the "refiner's fire" that produced pure spiritual metal in you.

Special Instructions

Formal training programs for new church officers are important, but
some have their limits. As a pastor who has met with scores of couples
preparing for marriage, I have often wondered if the premarital sessions
did any good. A mentoring process in addition to formal preparation
might be more effective over time.

Often new-officers' training focuses on the beliefs of the church, the
structure of the organization, and the "duties" of the office. Little attention is given to the development of prayer, discernment, deciding, and
acting in the heat of real ministry. For that reason I advocate an ongoing
preparation in the course of service. Clergy have a real opportunity to
grow and raise up leaders in the midst of shared ministry. But it won't
happen unless it is valued enough to be structured in. If it's not, the
press to "do" inevitably overwhelms the necessity to "be."

The new New Summit Church structures its board meetings with
one-third of the time allotted for training and enrichment, one-third for
worship and prayer, and one-third for decisions. They intend to stay that
course.

The six hundred board members queried by the Set Apart Lay
Leaders project were asked to identify the areas in which they felt they
had needed instruction as preparation for becoming elders. They were
then asked to identify the training they actually received prior to installation. Their responses and the corresponding "gaps" appear as following:[5]

	Need for	Received	Difference
Church documents	83%	75%	-8%
Church government	76%	71%	-5%
Organizational structure of board	71%	72%	+1%
History of Presbyterian Church	64%	57%	-7%
Sharing of faith	63%	50%	-13%
Presbyterian ethos	62%	46%	-16%

	Need for	Received	Difference
Doing evangelism	60%	30%	-29%
Care/shepherding skills	58%	29%	-29%
Reformed theology	56%	42%	-14%
Theological reflection	53%	25%	-25%
Group-building skills	53%	31%	-22%
The Bible	52%	34%	-18%
Conflict resolution	51%	23%	-28%
Leading prayer	48%	20%	-28%
Futuring	48%	22%	-26%
Decision making	46%	34%	-12%
Servant style leadership	45%	30%	-15%
History of congregation	42%	38%	-4%
Order of worship, liturgy	40%	44%	+4%
Teaching skills	35%	14%	-21%
Private prayer	34%	21%	-13%

Upon further analysis, we see the training gaps in clusters.

Structural–organizational	average of -4%
History	average of -9%
Biblical–theological–spiritual	average of -12%
Ministry skills	average of -21%
Effective meeting process	average of -23%

This again bears out the mechanical and procedural orientations that occupy the attention of many boards. It also reveals the need for a spiritual focus that extends to the life-giving process of meetings.

Jesus' model of teaching through action and reflection should be

noted. Throughout the day he and his disciples engaged people in ministry. Then they pulled back to reflect on what had happened. Jesus connected their experience with the Hebrew tradition. He taught them about
the nature of the kingdom. He equipped them with strategies for ministry. They prayed together for the kingdom's fulfillment in their midst.

We have asked people to serve as reflection givers at the conclusion
of meetings to provide the board with an opportunity to "unpack" the
meeting and learn from it. The unpacking includes theological reflection
upon the meeting. We encourage the pastor and presiding officer to be
part of a small agenda-design team that reflects upon the past meeting as
it prepares for the next.

Your Ritual Step to Covenant

As the ship of your board service prepares to set sail, realize that you
have been called by the faith community to be a "set apart" spiritual
leader in the church. You have said "yes" to the invitation. Your self-
appraisal has determined that you can bring only yourself, with your
humanness, unique faith story, and character. You are committed to a
disciplined life and have some clues about your gifts, even as you desire
a fuller expression of them. Now you are almost ready to take passage
for this new voyage. Stepping on to the boat requires preparation, examination, commitment, and one final thing: ritual.

When you are recognized or installed, you will enter into a covenant. That's appropriate because our identity as the people of God is
rooted in covenant. "I will be your God" and "you shall be my people"
form the very first covenant. Any freely associating community is held
together by a spoken or unspoken covenant. Business relationships rely
on written covenants or contracts. Even interpersonal relationships
(marriages) and small groups function best with clear understandings of
covenants and commitments.

In being "set apart," you as a candidate will be asked to make certain
promises. The community in turn promises respect, support, and encouragement. The more clearly these are stated, the better! They should be
clear enough to be reduced to writing, symbolized in art forms, and
included in a ritual. Unspoken assumptions will become problematic
downstream.

The covenants may include statements of belief, demarcations of relationships, identification of Christ's mission, spelled out duties, or even attitudes, such as "Will you serve the people with energy, intelligence, imagination, and love?"

You should be prepared to be set apart by ritual as well as by covenant. Some churches ordain by the laying on of hands. Some install through a covenant. Some commission with a charge. Some set apart through prayer or anointing.

Biblical precedents are rich. Moses commissioned Joshua through the laying on of hands (Num. 27:18–23). Samuel anointed David with oil (1 Sam. 16:13). In 1 Kings 19:19 Elijah cast his mantle over Elisha. Commissioning is important not only for the person being commissioned, but for the community as well—for in commissioning they share in the vision, commitment, and support of the ministry.

Jesus was commissioned by God in baptism. Deacons in the Greek church at Jerusalem were "set apart" as the apostles "prayed and laid their hands on them" (Acts 6:6). Paul and Barnabas: "appointed elders . . . with prayer and fasting they entrusted them to the Lord" (Acts 14:23). Paul reminded Timothy of his gift of prophetic utterance "with the laying on of hands by the council of elders" (1 Tim. 4:14).

The "setting apart" ritual should take place in a celebrative service. The service of ordination and installation should focus on Christ and on the joy and responsibility of serving him on the board. It should be personalized as much as possible for each individual, yet within the context of the lordship and purpose of Christ. Banquet, feast, and table all speak of celebration.

Let the service involve the whole parish. I remember one service in which balls of yarn in the four liturgical colors were passed through the church. Everyone was connected by holding the yarn during the "setting apart" prayers. Then the yarn was gathered and formed into a "yoke" that was placed around the neck of the person "set apart." This became an unforgettable symbolic stole!

Let your solemn vows and the joyous support of the congregation launch you on a delightful journey of spiritual leadership. Bon voyage!

CHAPTER 9

Entering the Stream: To New Board Members Being Assimilated into a Board

Having been selected, prepared, and installed, you are now ready to step into the boat. Along with others who are also new to the task of church governance, you will join board members who have been serving for one or more years.

Every good boat has a gangplank by which people can embark or disembark. I propose that gangplanks came into use because of the plethora of accidents that occurred when people tried to jump the gap between boat and dock. Even if a boat is moored tightly to the dock, the change from the sure footing of a pier to the unstable boat deck disorients new passengers.

Similarly, boards need to provide "gangplanks" to help newcomers bridge the gap to a new type of group experience. From studies of small groups, we know that every time an existing group is reconfigured, it becomes in fact a new group. Pastors and board leaders often forget that. They assume that if new board members know the duties of the office and the organizational structure of the board, they can fit right into the old scheme and begin to operate.

Stories: From a Cloud of Witnesses

A board begins a new life whenever new members are grafted in. Since the kind of boards we envision operate as close Christian communities, they, like families, need time to form as communities. The following listing of statements, collected from our survey of former board members, attests to community life on the board. We had asked, "What was your greatest reward or satisfaction?"

The variety of unique gifts and talents which we discovered in one another. It was always the exact blend of talents needed.

The feeling of closeness that developed among the members. Our church had been through a very trying time.

I was surprised at the respect I received as a member of the council.

I never thought I could be ready for the responsibility but learned that there was so much love and support to strengthen me and help my faith and talents.

The fellowship and deep friendship made during my term and which continues. I'm convinced that our retreats which were held early in the year established the bonding and was reinforced every regular meeting.

The work with fellow Christians in leadership roles for the betterment of the congregation, the church, and the creative Glory of God.

Having recently been widowed, I found a reason for living. It tightened my link with God. I found abilities long lost. I found how the church is operated and appreciated its methods.

Being part of a group that worked it out together.

A true sense of call by God to the office. The personal friendships and sense of trust and Christian respect that I gained from fellow elders was a real reward for me.[1]

The quality of friendship and community evident here did not happen by accident. Groups are formed through an intentional and sometimes difficult process. Groups go through a predictable life cycle. The cycle is most obvious in freely associating groups that are not bound by time constraints and structures. But the cycles appear even in the routine and development of well-organized groups such as boards and councils.

A Master Story: Seen through the Eyes of a Child

Before I offer insights about what you can expect in the development of
your board, let me retell a Bible story, found in John 5. It's the formation
of the disciples of Jesus into a ministry group. The small boy who gave
up his cakes and fish for the feeding of the multitude will tell the story.

My name is Benjamin. I live with my family in a village on
the Sea of Galilee, opposite from Capernaum. I may be just a kid,
but I keep by eyes open and ears to the ground, so I know what's
going on in my village. Jesus came to our area healing the sick and
teaching people about God. I used to listen to him and watch him
along with his disciples. Jesus would heal people during the day.
Then in the evening he would slip away to some remote spot with
his disciples. They spent a lot of time together. I suppose they were
resting and talking about what happened and who said what that day.

My parents got very interested in Jesus and became his followers. They liked what they heard and saw. One day when we were
with Jesus, the growing crowds kept him so busy that everyone lost
track of time. When supper time came, Jesus' disciples tried to shoo
us all toward home. Everyone was tired and hungry. I still had
some rolls and several fish left over from our family lunch. Suddenly in the commotion, Jesus asked for my bread and fish. So of
course I gave it to him. I'm not sure what happened after that. I
know that Jesus offered a blessing and the people had enough to eat.
In fact, there was plenty left over.

My dad thought it was a miracle! "Anyone who can feed five
thousand people is my kind of king," he said. Dad and some others
decided to approach Jesus and make him king, but Jesus slipped
away before they could get to him. He must have gone off again
with the twelve special disciples.

The next morning we couldn't find them. Their boats were
gone, so we figured they had returned to Capernaum overnight.
Everyone was excited. They gathered up all the boats they could
find and set sail. I'm glad my dad let me go along. "You could just
as well see what happens," he said.

We finally found Jesus on the other side. He was waiting for
us. He wanted to know if we had come because he put bread in our
bellies. Or were we really interested in a bread from heaven? The

discussion got pretty deep for me. I do know that Jesus did not want to be a king—at least not in the way my father was hoping.

Jesus made some strange claims about being the bread of life; he said that this bread would be broken in his death. Sounds really gross to me, but he invited my dad to eat this bread of his flesh and drink of his blood so that he would have life forever.

That was too much for Dad and many of his friends. They complained and objected. "It is too hard—too much for us," they said. They were disappointed and left him to return home. They said they couldn't continue to be his followers and disciples.

I stayed around for a while and overheard Jesus ask his disciples, "Will you also go away?" There was a long silence. The disciples seemed stunned. Finally the big fisherman spoke up: "Where else can we go? You have the words of eternal life. We have come to believe and know that you are the Holy One of God."

Jesus seemed relieved. They were going to stick together and work it out.

Dad was calling me. "Hurry, or you will miss the boat!" I ran to catch it. We never did see Jesus again, although we did hear about him. He caused quite a stir when he went to Jerusalem where he got killed. The big fisherman said he rose from the dead. I wonder . . .

Reflective Story Weaving

The bonding of the disciples into a community of faith, hope, and love reveals the stages of development through which groups go.

The disciples convened around an implicit rather than explicit covenant. They did not sign a contract on the dotted line. Jesus' "come, follow me and I will make you fishers . . ." was a pretty open-ended invitation. It left a lot of room for development.

The twelve invited to the inner circle were from various walks of life and represented many distinct personality types. Jesus took time with them to allow their stories to come out—along with their hopes and fears. As trust built up, they reflected on daily experiences together. Jesus kept tying what they were experiencing to the tradition—to Moses, David, Elijah, and Abraham—so they could make sense out of it and begin to form their own faith. He held before them a vision of "the kingdom of God," which provided direction for them.

Their initial successful and popular work of teaching and healing led to a certain euphoria. Then suddenly things began to fall apart. Who would have guessed that one of the Master's most dramatic miracles, the multiplication of the loaves and fish, would start the downhill slide? People began to question Jesus' leadership, wondering if he really knew what he was doing. Formerly faithful disciples fell away and abandoned ship. The twelve feared that their fellow disciples would join the others who had left, leaving Jesus to his own misguided fate.

In a moment of high anxiety, Jesus asked the twelve if they also wanted to go home. Peter responded with an affirmation of faith and hope, saying, in effect, that they could not make it on their own but would trust God for their lives. In that moment the group was born—not of their own effort, but by the gift of God's grace. Community came as gift.

Their covenant became explicit as the disciples prepared to be sent out two by two for ministry. They participated in ministry until they moved toward Jerusalem, where the group as they knew it died with the loss of its leader; its members returned home. Only an act of the power of God could give them cause for rebirth. Following the resurrection, the disciples were re-formed by the Spirit into a community that changed the world.

Stages of Board Development

Before a new group assembles for the first time, much work has gone on behind the scenes. Some form of invitation draws the group together. Generally the inviter functions as a convening leader. Those who respond hold the leader in high trust or esteem.

In the case of a church board, the selection process has been complex. I trust you have been offered considerable information so you know the nature and work of the board. But most of the information and personal contacts have been provided by a nominating committee or pastoral staff—people who may not be members of the board. As you now walk up the gangplank, you are being assembled for the first time as a group. The blending of faces and voices around the board table is new. You are ready for the first stage of group development.

Inclusion

The first stage of group life is inclusion. A friend who was an experienced leader of small groups observed, "No matter what you do in your group, the first six hours are spent sniffing. People ask, 'Is this a safe place for me to be?'" That is the reality of those first hours. You may fear that you will be exposed as stupid or inadequate for the task. You may fear that you may be manipulated or overpowered. This "safety" issue will be resolved only as all of you begin to build trust with one another. Don't assume trust will come automatically just because you all belong to the same church or have had associations with one another in the past.

A combination of self-disclosure, responsive hearing, and affirmation allows for the building of trust. In new relationships, self-disclosure begins with one's name, then moves to safe information about one's self, then to personal stories, then to one's hopes or fears. Sharing personal dreams and visions is often as risky as sharing problems and pain.

As new church leaders, you are not called together to share personal secrets, but your stories can bond you together as a board that is able to be open with one another—to come out and play, work, laugh, pray, and dream together.

Your first several gatherings should center more on group building than on decision making. An extended retreat at the beginning of your common life can provide this forum. But a word of caution: Many church-officer retreats are dominated by a heavy agenda of organizing, planning, goal setting, and making work assignments.

Whether they are used on a retreat or at a fellowship meal, at special meetings or during a dedicated time in your regular meeting, the following practices can help form the group.

Tell stories about the history of the church and about influential lay leaders who have gone before. When Loren Mead of The Alban Institute led one of our church session retreats, he asked the elders to form a straight line, ordering themselves by what year they became associated with the church. The line broke into clusters of three to five people who came to the church about the same time. In the group they discussed their "entrance stories" by identifying (1) the influences that led to their decision to be part of the church, (2) the laypeople who influenced them at that time, and (3) the qualities those leaders possessed. Each cluster then reported to the whole. Fascinating data came out about the history of the church, the "great cloud of witnesses," the nature of leadership, the power of personal influence, and people's faith commitment to God and the church.

Tell personal faith stories. No two stories are exactly the same. The Holy Spirit has used a rich variety of influences and experiences to bring each person to a relationship with God. Certainly there are common factors. When the stories are told, both the basic aspects of faith and the unique influences stand out. When your spirit bears witness with another's that you are both children of the heavenly Father, a bonding takes place at the deepest levels.

Self-disclosure is a beautiful gift that can foster intimacy and trust, but it can be troublesome if people are seduced or manipulated to go beyond the limits of their trust level with the group. I suggest that group leaders allow each person's inner trust indicator to determine that person's own level of self-disclosure.

Read the Bible together. The variety of ways people come to this Book is a testimony to its richness. It has tremendous value for intense study or personal devotional use. But it also can be used by a group that reads it together while attempting to relate personally to the story.

At one church I pastored I led one weekend retreat per month for parishioners at a retreat center. The format for all the large–group gatherings was group reading of the Exodus story: Israel's story of bondage, call, struggle, deliverance, wilderness journey, becoming a people, spiritual and administrative leadership, and gift of the promised land. We commented on what seemed interesting or significant, telling our own stories when they connected to the biblical story.

An occasional officers' retreat for Bible reading only, supplemented by worship and solitude, can be a powerful force for those in "set apart" ministries.

Call forth gifts. You are "set apart" because the church already has identified your special gifts for leadership. With that in mind, the first task of the newly forming board is to identify, make visible, and affirm your gifts. Though you may have some awareness of a gift or gifts, doubt and uncertainty may linger. One church officer could not bring himself to see himself as an "evangelist." Yet other board members pointed out how energetic and effective he was when inviting others and welcoming them to church! The council's affirmation will be a confidence builder.

As the gifts of all members are affirmed, the board becomes complete. God gives your board all the gifts it needs to fulfill its call. A member with the gift of humor will break the tension at the right time. One who discerns the mind of the group may formulate a concluding statement or motion. Another may serve as a historian to remind the group of its connection with past events or decisions. One who is tuned in to board members' feelings—helpfully naming them and sensitively slowing the group down to be sensitive to one another—may demonstrate pastoral gifts. (See appendix 3, "Identifying Natural Leadership.")

Pray for one another. Knowing that someone cares and prays for us is like stepping on an inviting welcome mat. Within your group try matching up prayer partners for a month or longer. Early in the board's term, take time to offer special prayers for the new members. Let each one identify a prayer or praise request to which the whole group can respond.

Pay attention to the "stuff" people bring into the gathering. Experience proves that if time is spent "logging in" at the beginning of the meeting, the agenda moves along at a much faster pace. "Connecting" is not a waste of time! It clears the air so that members can clearly consider the agenda without mixing it with their personal needs. It builds trust that opens communication lines and reduces potential conflicts.

Reflect on what happened in each gathering. Saint James Presbyterian Church in the Denver area closes each meeting (no matter how late) with a time to process the experience. It provides time to reflect on meanings, feelings, and accomplishments. If a person has been cut off, overpowered, or humiliated, an opportunity is given to minister and reconcile. This tack heads off parking-lot processing that does not always involve all the parties involved.

Worship the Lord. Placing all eyes upon the Creator, Savior, and Empowerer will draw the body together. Sing praise together, letting your voices tune to one another.

Elation

The second stage of group life is elation. An atmosphere of inclusion, through self-disclosure and a corresponding acceptance and affirmation, makes people feel safe. As trust continues to deepen, a certain elation sets in.

At this stage you will be pleased to experience the unity of the church—common faith, common beliefs and values, common purpose, and common needs. Sometimes this stage is called honeymoon or romance. Your internal feelings harmonize to the accompanying lyrics, "Isn't it nice that we are all so much alike!"

For this stage of board development, I suggest the following special, nonagenda gatherings for growth and development.

Extended time away in a retreat or conference setting. In such a setting routines are broken. The atmosphere is peaceful; distractions are minimized. The stage is set for creating new relationships and attitudes.

It is difficult to place a value on this experience. Some estimate that more spiritual growth can take place in one weekend away than in a year-long series of weekly gatherings. One survey, conducted among members, elders, and pastors, asked people in April 1982 to identify the settings in which their faith had been influenced. For all age groups, from teens through adults, a "camp-retreat" setting was the most frequently chosen response.[2] You may feel reluctant to spend the time and money for a retreat because it does not seem to be cost-effective. The old secular value that measures accomplishment in terms of productivity (what we make and do) is out of step with spiritual investment in being (what we become). There is no substitute for time away in retreat. Every board should schedule at least one annual retreat that includes no planning, deciding, or acting.

Several boards with which we are in contact have decided to move away from monthly evening meetings and substitute four working retreats a year; these provide time to go deeper in mutual fellowship, study, and deliberation.

The costs of a retreat are real, calculated in time away from family, travel expense and risk, and loss of rest. Even though the experience may have provided a change of pace and inspiration, people may come home more weary than when they left. Let the pace be easy. Vow to return participants more rested than when they arrived.

Jesus was in the habit of going away or taking the disciples for a night of prayer and reflection on the mountain. His practice served as a model for us. The Korean church's "prayer mountain," in which they go away for a Friday night prayer session in preparation for Sunday worship, is a model you might consider. One doesn't have to drive three hours one way, spend a hundred dollars, and have a weekend of nonstop meetings to do a retreat.

Sharing common meals provides another rich way to include new members and deepen the community and spiritual life of the group. The meals should be an intentional time for sharing and worship. Rather than allowing the conversation to drift from subject to subject (as in a dinner party), some basic structures could be set up to provide direction and make the meal an agape or love feast laced with worship.

One board meets every other month an hour before the meeting for a meal. One time during the salad course, someone read aloud Psalm 139 slowly and deliberately. Then informal dinner conversations covered "what we have been doing since the last meeting." During the main course, someone read Romans 12:1–2 and 9–21. Each person then selected one statement that was speaking to her and commented on it. The dessert was followed by shared prayers for the church, self, and others.

Special nonagenda meetings for the purpose of caring for one another, growing spiritually, and discussing agreed–upon themes help to build community. If the board meets monthly on Tuesdays, additional gatherings could be held four times a year on "fifth" Tuesdays. Some boards schedule an extra nonagenda gathering each month.

Of course, unity cannot be manufactured in structured gatherings alone. Working together, associating informally, and growing deep friendships all contribute to the elation of unity.

"Spiritual companion matches" challenge each member to grow. Dr. Howard Rice of San Francisco Theological Seminary said if he were starting a new church, he would place every elder under spiritual direction! This could initially be done by a pastor and eventually be moved to others who are qualified.

Disillusionment

The third stage of group life is disillusionment. At some point in the relationship, you will discover warts mixed in with the beauty spots. Suddenly, instead of singing about how much you are all alike, you add a verse that highlights your differences. Your admiration of and dependence on the leader may turn to second guessing the leader and pulling back. An unexpected crisis may make the group anxious, fearful that they may not "make it through." This crisis is normal, occurring in every relationship. Only a successful resolution of this dip in the bell curve can enable the group to move on toward its ultimate goal and destiny.

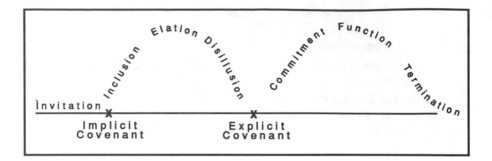

My book *Cultivating Religious Growth Groups* provides further elaboration on the life cycle of a group in terms of process and group dynamics [3]

But the classic theological treatment on disillusionment is provided by Dietrich Bonhoeffer in his book *Life Together.* Bonhoeffer speaks out of the context of an underground seminary in Nazi Germany. He begins by quoting Psalm 133:1: "Behold, how good and how pleasant it is for brethren to dwell together in unity!" (KJV). "Amen," people would shout in the elation stage of a group's life. But Bonhoeffer soon bursts that bubble.

> Innumerable times a whole Christian community has broken down because it had sprung from a wish dream. The serious Christian, set down for the first time in a Christian community, is likely to bring with him a very definite idea of what Christian life together should be and to try to realize it. But God's grace speedily shatters such dreams. Just as surely as God desires to lead us to a knowledge of genuine Christian fellowship, so surely must we be overwhelmed by a great disillusionment with others, with Christians in general, and, if we are fortunate, with ourselves. By sheer grace, God will not permit us to live even for a brief period in a dream world. He does not abandon us to those rapturous experiences and lofty moods that come over us like a dream. God is not a God of the emotions but the God of truth. Only that fellowship which faces such disillusionment, with all its unhappy and ugly aspects, begins to grasp in faith the promise that is given to it. The sooner this shock of disillusionment comes to an individual and to a community the better for both. A community which cannot bear and cannot survive such a crisis, which insists upon keeping its illusion when it should be shattered,

permanently loses in that moment the promise of Christian community. Sooner or later it will collapse. Every human wish dream that is injected into the Christian community is a hindrance to genuine community and must be banished if genuine community is to survive. He who loves his dream of a community more than the Christian community itself becomes a destroyer of the latter, even though his personal intentions may be ever so honest and earnest and sacrificial.

Bonhoeffer has asserted that our salvation does not come through our own efforts. Neither does community come by our own resources or like-mindedness. It comes as a gift, for:

A Christian comes to others only through Jesus Christ. . . . Without Christ we also would not know our brother, nor could we come to him. The way is blocked by our own ego.

But the disillusionment does serve a purpose:

Thus the very hour of disillusionment with my brother becomes incomparably salutary, because it so thoroughly teaches me that neither of us can ever live by our own words and deeds, but only by that one Word and Deed which really binds us together—the forgiveness of sins in Jesus Christ. When the morning mists of dreams vanish, then dawns the bright day of Christian fellowship.[4]

I recommend that every three years church boards read and discuss the first twenty-two pages of *Life Together*. Without facing the reality of disillusionment, they will limp along playing games or live only as a human community, devoid of spiritual power.

I mentioned earlier in this book that some people come off boards with a bitter taste in their mouths. Their expectation of a spiritually enriching experience has not been realized. Let's face it: We disappoint each other out of our own human efforts. Pastors may disappoint you. Board members may disappoint each other. You may disappoint pastors. Our failure to process our disappointments theologically in light of God's grace often leaves us bitter. Once you accept God's gift of community, confessing that the board is held together only by God's love, you can live in joy and thankfulness—getting on with your high calling. Then the common spiritual disciplines will have a solid foundation.

Commitment

The fourth stage of group life is commitment. The leader cannot carry
the group. Wishful thinking will not accomplish anything. Illusions
about our own abilities and efforts have been deflated. In spite of our
differences, new life begins.

When you first entered the board room, the covenant for the group
was implicit or assumed. After working through the time of struggle,
when you may have pulled away from the original leadership, you are
now prepared to enter into an explicit covenant. You commit together
to work for the purpose of the board and to share in its leadership. Leaders will still be necessary, but members will no longer be dependent or
counterdependent.

The new glue of the covenant of grace and love will bind your board
together, allowing you to sail on toward a common goal.

Anticipating the Next Stages

We have taken you through the first four stages of group development.
When you have come—by God's grace—to common trust and commitment, you are ready to sail. In the next chapter we will explore the
functioning stage of working together on the board toward common
goals. Then in the final chapter we will look at the terminating stage—
preparing to exit the ship and reinvest energies elsewhere.

CHAPTER 10

Rowing the Boat:
To Active,
Established Board Members

You are now on board. I hope you crossed the gangplank safely. I trust your "new" board is forming itself as a community of faith. Now is the time to take hold of your oar and pull—to power and steer the boat. In this chapter I will introduce you to the way boards and councils function and ways you can be an effective, participating member.

Some Stories: Three Epistles

Our board stories come in the form of three letters.

Pat Knutson is the new president of the church council at Overland Park Lutheran. The first year this council worked with our project to integrate spirituality and administration in their board meetings, the going was slow. Now, at the beginning of the second year, Pat has just returned from a council retreat. She writes,

> I'm enclosing a copy of the agenda from our meetings. The council format is working well. It may still evolve more, but for the moment everyone is okay with it. What the paper doesn't tell is what really happens during the discussions. In May we came to what I call an *enthusiastic consensus* on our refurbishing efforts as a council. We still have work to do with the congregation, but I think we're moving!
>
> The retreat held that Saturday was in some ways a continuation of the council meeting—at least as far as excitement is concerned! You can see that our topic was spirituality. Everyone had an hour for individual reflection, study, and meditation. I was a bit nervous

about how they would react. As we closed the meeting day and did some reflection, everyone was excited about that time. It was a great retreat!

I guess all of this is the long way to say that "worshipful work" really does work rather nicely. Thanks to your project for being a resource that helped us get started. It's exciting to ponder where it will lead.[1]

Pastor Jim Belt wrote about a reorganization of the meeting agenda at Underwood Hills Church in Omaha.

Several years ago we came to the conclusion that our board meetings were often unfocused because we conducted them with sequential reporting. The clerk would report and in the reporting be active and animated, and everyone else would be passive and reflective. The next person to report would be the treasurer. Again, the treasurer would be active and animated; everyone else would be passive, reflective, critical, etc.

We discovered that this particular sequential process of filling the session's docket took out the majority of the elders from making the meeting "click," and so we condensed the reporting function into the first 25% of the session docket and took the remaining hour and one half, divided it into two sections of 45 minutes each, used the first 45 minute section to discuss what needs to be the emphasis in the life of the church in the next three months, and to a lesser extent the next six, and then to even a lesser extent the next nine. The last 45 minutes of the meeting are devoted to how the different committees could participate in carrying out these emphases. That has resulted in a dramatic change in the life of the church, because during that hour and a half every elder is an active participant, sort of the difference between baseball and football.[2]

Pastor Mike Beaugh told this story about the Beacon Hills Presbyterian Church in San Antonio at our recent collegium.

Our ninety-six-year-old once large, prosperous congregation took steps toward redevelopment in 1986. By 1990, it became obvious that a piece of the redevelopment had to be a rethinking of the role of elected church leaders. They felt overworked and frustrated, overwhelmed by the administrative minutiae, dissatisfied with their lack of meaningful accomplishment. Burnout, stunted imaginations, and stillborn ideas were the order of the day. In candid and open conversations, all agreed that something had to give.

We took some steps toward revitalizing leadership. We appointed a task force to study the problem and find solutions. The task force struck on a novel idea. It decided to go to the sources for guidance. The sources were Scripture and our denomination's *Book of Order*.

The task force approached the sources with several questions: What did leaders in the scriptural stories do? What was their role in the faith community? What does the *Book of Order* require of congregational leaders? Does either source require the kind of structure that seemed to be strangling the leadership of our church?

The research bore fruit—several revelations:

1. Leaders in the scriptural stories were called out by God to nurture the members of the faith community in the spirit of Christ (Acts 20 and 1 Peter 5). This was their primary job.

2. All members of the faith community—not just the leaders—were considered ministers with gifts for ministry (Romans 12 and 1 Corinthians 12).

3. The *Book of Order* does not require any one way to organize the work of a Presbyterian church aside from the requirement of having a session responsible for the life of the congregation. This responsibility can be delegated.

4. Leaders in the scriptural stories sought out gifted members and commissioned them for specific tasks (Acts 15).

As a result of this research we began to reorganize the work of our leaders. Spiritual leadership would be the primary role of the session. Most of the administrative and program responsibilities were placed in the hands of nonboard members, leaving the board freer to concentrate on such things as vision and direction for the congregation, long-range planning, and communication with members of the congregation.

Several practical outcomes resulted. The board was reduced in size from twenty-four to twelve members, and quarterly Saturday meetings replaced the monthly Tuesday meetings.[3]

At this point in your board history, your own story about how your board functions will be somewhat limited. A year from now you will have a story to tell. I realize that you have had little influence on how the board approaches its work. You can, however, play an important role. You can hold before your pastor and board a vision of worshipful work as the organizing and energizing principle of the board. You can interpret the thesis of this book to those who plan and process the agenda. You can be open to and prepared for practices that build the common life of the board and root its life in worship. Your openness to prayerful gatherings will exert some pressure on an oar that steers the boat in a worshipful direction.

A Master Story: Primed and Sent

Let me complement Pat's, Jim's, and Mike's stories with the master story found in Luke 10. It's told in the voice of a "follower" at a leadership seminar led by Jesus.

> You don't know my name because I was not chosen to be one of the twelve. But I've been around as long as they have and believe in Jesus and the kingdom he talks about. One day Jesus told us he had a plan. He wanted to visit a number of villages and wanted to send his followers two by two to live in those villages to prepare for his coming. I volunteered to go. He said "okay" but insisted that I get some training along with the other sixty-nine he had invited. The training seminar lasted all day and we covered a lot of material. Here is a summary of what he taught us:
>
> "The harvest is plentiful, but the laborers are few; therefore ask the Lord of the harvest to send out laborers into his harvest. Go on your way. See, I am sending you out like lambs into the midst of wolves. Carry no purse, no bag, no sandals; and greet no one on the road. Whatever house you enter, first say, 'Peace to this house!' And if anyone is there who shares in peace, your peace will rest on that person; but if not, it will return to you. Remain in the same house, eating and drinking whatever they provide, for the laborer deserves to be paid. Do not move about from house to house. Whenever you enter a town and its people welcome you, eat what is set before you; cure the sick who are there, and say to them, 'The kingdom of God has come near to you.' But whenever you enter a

town and they do not welcome you, go out into its streets and say, 'Even the dust of your town that clings to our feet, we wipe off in protest against you. Yet know this: the kingdom of God has come near' (vv. 2-11).

So off we went. It was scary at first. But we were amazed at what happened when we healed and taught in the name of Jesus. When we all got back together for debriefing, I told Jesus, "Lord, in your name even the demons submit to us!" He was so happy. He said he watched Satan fall from heaven like a bolt of lightning—then reminded us about the new authority he had given to us. Then he broke into a song of thanksgiving to God for what God had revealed and given to us—mere babes. Not even prophets and kings have seen what I was privileged to see!

Reflective Story Weaving

As I weave the three contemporary stories with this master story, I am struck with the dimension of *leadership as character*. If visionary leaders are called to wear or bear the vision, character must surely come into play. You may bring a lot to the new board—experience in management, educational qualifications, and personal skills, but if the vision of the kingdom is not integrated into the fabric of your very being, the character dimension will be missing. In each of our three contemporary stories in this chapter, a quality of corporate character was emerging in the boards being transformed. The follower's story raises the same themes. "I send you out as lambs in the midst of wolves." What a contrast in characters!

Two distinct types of character—wolflike and lamblike—can operate in a board room; both may claim to lead in the name of Jesus. Let's allow this story to provide insight about which one you and your board will model itself after.

Work Together

Work together in the name of Christ. The "lambs" were sent in pairs. Jesus knew the dangers of isolation and of "Lone-Rangerism." Mutual planning, prayer, and support are essential in boards. Your best work and decisions will take place on a foundation of fellowship. Sheep stay together. If one breaks from the pack, the whole herd will follow. Wolves may run in packs, but they are so competitive that they generally operate alone. Sheeplike leaders enter into ministry together, being both supportive of and accountable to one another.

Work in Confidence

Work in confidence that Christ has gone before you to prepare the way. "The Lord of the harvest" sends you into the fields that God has planted and nourished. Wolflike characters roam about waiting to take advantage of others—even using trends and theories to gain leverage in an argument. Wolves will not pay attention to fences and boundaries. They are calculating, conniving, and sly, looking to take advantage for their own gain. Lamblike characters, on the other hand, stay in the field chosen by the guiding eye of the shepherd. Look for signs of the presence of Christ as you listen to and love the people both inside and outside the church. This will demand attentive listening. Where has Christ already set up a situation that is ripe for ministry? Your board will want to join him there.

Depend on the Gifts and Presence

Depend on the gifts and presence of God to do what you cannot make happen on your own. "Take no shoes . . . no lunch bag . . . no purse." Lambs possess very little equipment—offensive or defensive. That makes them extremely vulnerable. They trust their protector and provider. Jesus taught about the responsibility of the good shepherd, likening himself to him and asking his disciples to deny themselves.

The Quakers speak of the "cumber" of life—the attachments that hold us down and inhibit our free, responsive movement. Their philosophy contrasts with current American culture, which is obsessed with gathering, using, consuming, amassing, and then trying to protect what we have. Jesus said to the lambs, "Don't greet anyone on the road." That is, don't get yourselves so tied up and boxed in with your socializing that your movement is inhibited.

The wolf is well equipped: Ears pick up a wide range of sound from a distance. Eyes fasten on the slightest movement. Nose responds to the scent of others. Legs outrace the prey. Fangs make the kill and tear the victim into bite sizes for devouring.

On occasions, church leaders operate more like wolves than lambs. Recently I saw a bus with "Christians in Action" written on its side just above what appeared to be a vicious, roaring lion! Given the committee and program structures of many boards, it is easy for board members to slip into a pattern of defending and protecting their programs and budgets against other competing committees; they might better be seeking the good of the whole church. Limited funds and volunteer resources add to the potential defensive behaviors. Both Mike's and Jim's boards had fallen into that trap. Beating the competition off rather than working cooperatively with the church down the street exhibits another wolflike behavior.

Good boards, as well as good board members, demonstrate a degree of vulnerability. They do not have to be superorganized, have all the answers, and have the slickest promotion to reach their goals. The servant who leads the way forward is much more akin to the lamb. This does not give license for sloppy planning. You will still have to work hard to be prepared. You need to listen to the church and to one another. You will struggle to discern the will of God. In the Matthew account of this same story, Jesus adds a line. "I am sending you out like sheep into the midst of wolves; so be wise as serpents and innocent as doves" (10:16). Wise "sheep" do their homework. But the innocence with which you work attests to your vulnerability and determination to work in an honest, straightforward manner.

Identify with People in Friendship

Identify with people in friendship. Jesus instructed his disciples to say peace to a house they entered. They were to stay in and eat at a blessed house, not moving around from house to house. Lamblike leadership identifies with people, listening to them, and hearing their stories. They touch and feel the hurt. Wolves, on the other hand, are on the prowl, moving around—luring people out of their houses so they can take advantage of them when they are vulnerable. "No," Jesus says. "Live in the midst of the people." Mike's board became lambs when they decided to become elders-in-touch.

Joyce and I wanted to invest in people through the vehicle of the meal. We created a simple meal event and called it Table Grace. It was not a prayer meeting, not a social evening, not a Bible study session, and not a dinner party. It was more like a love feast (an agape meal).

As guests gathered, we lit a candle to acknowledge the presence of Christ. The reading of an evening psalm preceded the breaking of a common loaf of freshly baked bread. During bread-breaking, each person expressed some aspect of thanks. Then while we continued to share stories, we snacked on finger foods—mostly vegetables. A gospel reading, followed by silence, led to the serving of a bowl of soup. Over soup, the conversations ranged far and wide. As the soup bowls were cleared, our guests were invited to identify concerns so prayers could be offered on their behalf. After the prayers, we passed raw fruit. A simple blessing concluded the evening.

You as a board member could create and host your own Table Grace. Our Christian liturgies started at tables in houses. A short step can return us there.

Engage in a Ministry of Healing

"Heal the sick," said Jesus. Wolves are not healers. Wolves are carnivorous, taking life to maintain their own life. They diminish victims, taking something very precious away from them. Wolflike leaders think, *For me to be a somebody, you must be made to be less than somebody—a nobody*. They put others down, jockeying for position and advantage, trying to get an edge in order to overpower. They take away life.

Jesus spoke harshly of the evangelists of his day. "Woe to you, . . . For you cross sea and land to make a single convert, and you make the new convert twice as much a child of hell as yourselves" (Matt. 23:15). These evangelists, whom the Lord called "hypocrites," were successful in making converts, but they then imprisoned these converts in their unloving ecclesiastical systems. They rescued people from one bondage and placed them in another. Glorying in their status as evangelists, they fed on the power they exercised over new converts. They diminished rather than enhanced the lives of new followers.

Wolflike leadership lords it over others. By contrast, the authority that Jesus gives is not for the purpose of lording it over others but for the purpose of being the genuine servant who builds up another.

Lambs possess the spirit of healers. In league with the shepherd they cleanse wounds, provide rest and support, and stay "with" the sick while God heals. They are at ease.

Wolves growl "grrr," which comes from a tense jaw and throat. "Baa" comes from an open, relaxed throat. As a jogger, I know what happens to me when I am surprised by a loud, threatening "grrr." My heart rate increases. The hair on the back of my neck stands up. I increase my rate of speed to get away. I don't want to be around a "grrr." But if I run past a surprising "baa" from a sheep, I will smile and wave— maybe even move closer for a look. Running past a new home construction site one day, I heard a voice from the roof: "A bit faster, man." Looking up, I saw a bearded Amish shingler smiling at me. I waved back; his lamblike mannerism was refreshing in contrast to the way some might urge one to "run faster!"

Given the amount of conflict that tears the fabric of churches today, your board members may be called upon to be healers. The internal conduct of the board at meetings needs to be peaceable, so that all members are valued and built up. But you must also reach beyond your own table to the pockets of alienation and discord within your congregation. The more deliberate and skilled councils are at conflict resolution, the healthier the whole church can become.

Announce the Gospel

Opportunities will come for you as a board to announce the gospel. Often boards are silent on this count. Jesus follows his mandate to heal with the mandate to speak. "Say to them, the kingdom of God has come near" this place. Yet only about one-fourth of the members of our churches ever utter a "baa." We tend to be silent people. If we continue to operate this side of the "sound barrier," we will continue to decline in membership. Boards can send powerful gospel messages when they speak a united word of witness. In reporting to the congregation or to the world, they can say, "we took this course of action because we believe. . . ."

Jesus sets up the sequence: Do the work; then speak the word. Both are important. The work earns us the right to speak.

Accept and Learn from Failure

When the "lambs" were not welcomed in a town, they were instructed to shake the dust off their feet and move on. But they were still to announce, "The kingdom of God has come near you." This was the same "baa" proclamation Jesus had instructed following successful healings. From the human perspective, the rejections were failures. In the economy of God's kingdom, nothing was lost and the gospel had been proclaimed.

How do lambs and wolves face failure? Wolves blame or act guilty and cowardly. If you say, "Bad dog!" to your collie, it will drop its ears, lower its head, put its tail between its hind legs, and sulk off into a corner. But if you say, "Bad lamb!" to a sheep, it will just stand there and look at you. It may have a tail (most are cut off at birth because they cannot be controlled and collect dirt), but it can't get it between its legs.

Jesus says to his sheep, "If they reject you, they reject me and the One who sent me," so put things in perspective. Your worth and value as a child of God do not hinge on your personal success or on your board's success. It won't be the first time the gospel has been rejected. Don't get stuck. "Shake off the dust." Know when to move on into more productive work, leaving the perceived failures with God, where they belong.

Live Graciously with Success

Live graciously with success. If wolves are successful, do they quit eating? No. They keep on hunting. Their appetite can never be completely satisfied. They are consumed by desire. The mystics and saints in the church often comment on the appetite of desire. Desires are selfish, possessive, entangling, and complex. The Christian disciplines instruct us that desires are to be fulfilled only in union with Christ. We are restless until we rest "in him," as Augustine said. The desire is not to be suppressed or destroyed, but purified and transformed in Christ. Wolves never have enough—never enough power, control, or guarantees. Desire among lambs is fulfilled in Jesus Christ. Their "baa" says, "All I want is to know him, to love him, and to live to the glory of God."

Our master story from Luke 10 concludes with a word about the lamblike leaders: "You have hidden these things from the wise and the

intelligent [the wolves] and have revealed them to infants" [the lambs]
(v. 21).

Verse 17 provides a note of joy: "The seventy returned with joy."
Jesus rejoiced and gave thanks to God. Glance back at the beginning of
this chapter and the letter from Pat. Notice how genuinely excited that
council was. They were discovering the joy of the reality that Jesus
named and blessed. Kings and prophets had not seen it, but the disciples
had. And so had Pat's council. That same reality is open to your board.

Don't misunderstand. I am not suggesting that you participate in a
passive way as a lamblike leader on your board. No, I want you to see
yourself and others on the board as people of strength whose servant-
style leadership makes a powerful difference. A board should be open to
using each person's strength and experience "to the max." Your strength
can be shared, used in flexible ways to empower you as a person in light
of the needs and tasks of the council.

Implementing Ministry

Committee structures can be empowering, if they free members to focus
their energies on particular tasks or ministries. But I have seen a lot of
frustrated committee members who felt they were not placed in positions
of responsibility that drew upon their best gifts and lively interests. They
were not able to offer their best because they were not given the opportunity or because a controlling pastor would not allow opinions, decisions,
and skills of the board members to emerge. We still search for ways to
empower each board member to contribute his or her best.

One example of this open effort comes from Episcopal Bishop Jack
Wyatt. He describes an attempt to organize a new deliberative group
around both community and task. After delineating what their community, leadership, and task needs were, group members took time to introduce themselves to one another in the context of one of these three
phrases: (1) why I said yes to this call; (2) what I have to offer to these
particular tasks; (3) what you have to look out for in working with me.
Bishop Wyatt says,

> If there is anything that I've learned in this process, it is that com-
> munity is built by paying exquisite attention to each individual
> rather than primarily to the organization. A human being is of more

importance than any structure. Once one's basic needs for belong-
ing and having influence are adequately addressed, one can give
oneself to share in developing the common vision which defines our
corporate task.[4]

As this organizing effort continued under Wyatt's direction, each
board task was placed as a heading on a separate page of large newsprint,
with open space left below for names to be added. Each member wrote
the names of members under a task for which they seemed, in light of the
introductions, to have the greatest gifts. (Every member was to place
every board member, including herself, on one sheet.)
 From this exercise the board chose a likely lead person and a primary support person for each task, based at first on whose name appeared most frequently on the sheet. If that person agreed to take the
lead, she identified another person on the sheet whom she most wanted
as a primary support person. These selections were tentative, pending
further discussion and negotiation.
 Each lead person kept the list of names listed under the task and
later called on them if more support was needed. This provided a pool
from which personnel could be drawn as each task came to the fore.
 You see here a flexible model that is responsive to needs; at the
same time it empowers council members to use their best gifts. If you
get locked into an unproductive committee, you might want to suggest
this method to your board's leadership.

Conclusion

Taking hold of the right oar, pulling in concert with others, and using
your best efforts are all needed as the boat called *council* makes its
way—governing and ordering the life, worship, and ministries of the
church. All the while it is being carried on the waters of the Lord of the
church, who is working out God's purposes.

CHAPTER 11

Nearing the Shore: To Board Members Preparing to Exit a Board

Your term of office is about up. You near the shore and prepare to make your exit. This may be the most important time of your whole board ride, so let's consider how to make the most of it. Listen to the experience of board members across the country who were asked, "What satisfaction did you derive from your service on the board?"

Stories and Stats: Telling It Like It Is

The camaraderie shared by board members—all ages and backgrounds. My spiritual life was enhanced and my commitment deepened. The last three months of my tenure I thought I was more than ready to get off. Now I realize I will miss it!!!

None. I have been left with grave skepticism and feel very devalued, cynical, and discouraged. I don't feel that I was valued for my opinions and left with a bad feeling regarding the church. There was great resistance toward examining important controversial issues in any serious way; resistance to change, and Bible studies, etc.

My time on the session was very positive and rewarding for me. I never regretted saying "yes" when they asked me. The greatest reward was the feeling of doing God's work and the satisfaction that goes with that. I will serve again in the future.

Exhilaration, inspiration, participation—was a good, happy, experience.

Right now, very little. Six years of my treatment has left me bitter and angry. It's hurtful to have pastors encourage your efforts to your face and fail to support you in front of others . . . and fail to assign anyone else to my committee—leaving you a committee of one person with no board support.

This completed my second term. At the end of the first term I vowed never to be on the board again. At the end of this term, I would respond "yes" if called again! This board was encouraged to be about God's work. When I list "great events" in my life, serving on the session will be high on the list.

In my first term I had a "good" feeling. In this latest term there is not a "good" feeling. I trust God will show me the way to endure the remainder of this term under this pastor.

To fulfill a service which I hope honored God and helped fulfill the mission of Jesus Christ. We were blessed with a strong session of true believers and disciples who could think for themselves, were concerned about doing God's work, and were great examples. I do think I'll come back to service next as a deacon. I sense that's where God's work will really get done.[1]

The composite story of the personal effect of board service on six hundred former board members can be told in table form:[2]

	Agree	Agree/Disagree	Disagree
Gained greater access to information about denomination	83%	13%	4%
Learned to trust God	83%	14%	3%
Gained greater understanding of how the denomination works	79%	17%	4%
Strengthened my love for God	79%	17%	4%

	Agree	Agree/Disagree	Disagree
Grew in understanding of what it means to be a Christian	77%	17%	6%
Established a closer relationship with the pastor	75%	14%	12%
Gained greater understanding of the church of Jesus Christ	82%	21%	7%
Learned to tolerate diversity within the congregation	82%	23%	5%
Gained a greater appreciation of church polity	66%	24%	10%
Gained greater self-confidence in my work off the session	65%	23%	12%
Learned how groups can come to agreement	60%	30%	10%
Increased ability to make tough decisions	57%	28%	14%
Learned to tolerate diversity within the denomination	52%	36%	12%
Feel burned out, tired, and weary	29%	26%	45%
Confidence in the denomination has diminished	20%	20%	60%
Confidence in the congregation has diminished	12%	14%	74%

A Master Story: Letting Go

We will revisit these composite stories later when we weave them with a master story. For that story, based on Genesis 32, we listen to Rachel, wife of the patriarch Jacob.

> When I first met Jacob, I fell in love with him immediately. He had been sent away to our land by his parents to look for a wife. Besides, he needed to get away from his brother who had threatened to kill him. I soon learned that Jacob was quite a conniver. He had cheated his twin brother Esau out of the family birthright. He and my father were always at each other—seeing who could take advantage of the other. It caused no small problems in our house. Jacob ended up with both my sister and me as his wives, and a good share of the family wealth besides!
>
> He sensed that God was calling him to return to his native land, which God had promised to his ancestors. But as far as he knew, Esau was still a threat to kill him. We started our journey. As we approached Esau's region, Jacob sent gifts ahead to his brother. The night before we were to meet Esau, Jacob sent us across the stream and stayed by himself for the night. He was very afraid and fidgety. The next morning he returned to us with a pronounced limp. When I asked him what happened, he said something about wrestling with an angel from God. In the fight the angel hurt Jacob's hip. But when Jacob had the angel pinned down, Jacob said, "I will not let you go until you bless me." The blessing must have stuck, because my husband is a different man—no longer a conniving cheater, but a gracious man of God. In fact, he was given a new name, Israel. Things turned out well. The next day Esau welcomed him home. The brothers were reconciled.

Reflective Story Weaving

Rachel's story brings to mind an experience I had with a small group. Over three years our group experienced a number of significant "moments" as we struggled together to grow in our faith and support one another. When the covenant renewal time drew near, we sensed that our growth and callings were leading in different directions. We struggled with the decision but finally concluded that the group should be terminated.

In our last gathering we sat together in a circle on the floor and entered into a "blessing" service. We read the story of Jacob's wrestling with an angel—agreeing that we, like Jacob, "would not let you go until you bless me." One by one the members identified (1) how the group experience had been a wrestling with God and one another, (2) how it had left its mark on them, and (3) what blessing they sought before departure. Group members responded to one another. It was a powerful, moving conclusion to our life. One member, in fact, said, "Isn't it interesting; when we finally decided not to be a group any longer, we became one!"

The Terminating Stage of Group Life

In chapters 9 and 10, I purposely did not complete the life-cycle-of-a-group sequence. I took you as far as the functioning stage, where a group operates in accord with its stated purpose and goals. But that comes to an end, and groups, following the rhythm of nature itself, also die. Their life cycles go full circle. Though a group dies, a seed remains that can be the source of continuing life.

Here are some glimpses of the distilled wisdom that settles from the weaving of these stories: (1) Life cycles are part of the order of creation. (2) God is in the struggle within the process of board life. (3) God has power to transform and shape boards. (4) Involvement on a board carries risk for pain and hurt. Healing is often needed. (5) Great learnings await members toward the end of their term. (6) The spiritual discipline of "letting go" is a friend toward the end.

Your council dies an annual death. When it reconstitutes with several new faces, it is a new group. Now that you are leaving the boat and walking the gangplank marked "exit," you need to prepare for your departure. Prepare to adjust, grieve, and discern what your next calling will be.

I am struck with the power for growth, change, and wisdom that can come in the "last days" of a relationship. It's similar to what can happen in the last few minutes of a counseling session: The counselor has set a time limit for a session with a counselee. The limit creates a compact "end zone" when so much comes out. I marvel at the wisdom sometimes condensed into a few statements uttered on deathbeds. In the same way, the last few meetings on a board can be the best. Prepare for them.

Hospice care for the dying offers insights for those who face a "little death." Those who work with the dying give advice as follows:

Put Your House in Order

Wrap things up so that those who are responsible for your affairs can see clearly what needs to be done when you are gone. The same is true in boards, especially if you have carried significant committee responsibilities. Leave good records of what you have done. Take time to reflect creatively with others about what you have learned. What worked and what didn't work? Why? Why not? If your committee needs to make a hard and sensitive decision, should it be made before you leave? Leave your work in the shape you would like to inherit it if you were new to the board.

Forgive Old Grudges

Don't carry them to your grave. They will continue to eat away at your life and energy. You may need to forgive someone whether or not that person knows it. You may need to ask forgiveness from a fellow member as well. Break clean.

Say Thank You

You have been on this boat for a good long trip. Others have pulled oars with you. Considering the significant fellowship that has been generated, there should be many possibilities for thanks-giving.

The Exit Interview

Earlier in this book I indicated that very few churches conduct exit interviews with departing board members. The press of orientation and organization of a new board tends to consume the energies of board leaders, leaving you who exit to walk the plank alone and self-adjust to life on the other side of the stream. An exit interview team should be available to sit down with you. Such a team should include a pastor, an officer of the council, and one or two people of your choice.

In our elder survey, 19 percent said that no acknowledgment was given at the conclusion of their term of office. Only 2 percent indicated that a formal interview was held. Of those who had been acknowledged, 46 percent had been thanked by the pastor at the last meeting, and 26 percent had been thanked at a ritual in a morning worship service. Sixteen percent had been invited to participate in a retreat with newly elected elders, and 15 percent had been asked to consider some other active church leadership role.[3]

The purpose of a formally scheduled exit interview is twofold—for the good of the board and for your own good.

Interview Helps Board

It provides a way for the board to give thanks to you for what is often a thankless job. The thanks can affirm the particular gifts and abilities you have offered. You may not have been aware that a gift was useful. Anecdotes should be cited that illustrate your contribution: "Remember when . . . " In this context the story telling we have been advocating continues. The interviewers should also glean your perspectives on the organization of the board and the process of its meetings. Perhaps board leaders don't schedule exit interviews for fear they might hear how boring or unproductive the meetings can be!

We asked our six hundred exiting board members, "In your opinion, were constructive meetings impeded by any of the following?" They responded:[4]

	Yes	No
Lack of information	52%	48%
Domination by a few vocal persons	46%	54%
Conflict	40%	60%
Hurried decisions	38%	62%

	Yes	No
Absence of a vision for the future	28%	72%
Pastoral style of leadership	28%	72%
Poorly prepared committee reports	25%	75%
Domination by the pastor	20%	80%
Lack of purpose	18%	82%

We also asked, "What factors made serving on the session difficult?"[5]

	Agree	Agree/Disagree	Disagree
Long, unproductive meetings	31%	24%	45%
Heavy workload of session	30%	26%	45%
Dominance by a few members	29%	20%	51%
Congregation's complaints about what the session was or was not doing	27%	23%	50%
Dominance by pastor	19%	19%	62%
Lack of theological knowledge	18%	24%	58%
Lack of knowledge about Presbyterianism	14%	26%	60%
Backbiting among session members	12%	16%	72%
Lack of freedom to speak up in meetings	11%	14%	75%

Departing members' responses to exit interview questions like the ones compiled above can produce a wealth of helpful information. So can responses to more open-ended questions: What surprised you about your service on the board? What was fulfilling for you? What was missing for you? Good boards have a feedback loop. Exit interviews should be in that loop.

Interview Helps Exiting Member

The exit interview's second purpose focuses on the exiting person—that's you. What has been the effect of the experience on the board for you? You need an opportunity to formulate your responses via some open reflection time with others who care about you.

The Effect of Board Service

Returning to the statistical table near the beginning of this chapter, we asked departing board members how the term of office had affected them personally. Of the top five responses, two involved gaining understanding and access to information about the denomination. Three of the top responses related to love for and trust in God and growing in understanding of what it means to be a Christian. A narrative response to an open-ended question confirmed this; 125 out of 512 indicated their greatest satisfaction had to do with the transcendent or the spiritual.

Other significant effects of service were relational—close fellowship with other elders and the pastor. Personal growth and confidence followed. Twenty-nine percent reported they left burned out, tired, and weary.

You may be asked how (if at all) your statement of faith differs from the faith statement you made upon entry. Where was God's presence apparent to you? We have said that the board table is a locus for spiritual formation. Has that happened for you? In what way? This would be a good time to update your faith story.

You may also be given opportunity to reflect upon your love and hope for the church. What signs of life do you see in it? What signs of decay do you perceive? Do you hold visions for it that the board was unable or unwilling to address? What will we do about those "capped" visions? Where should they be laid? What is unfinished that needs attention?

Leaving Clean

To leave clean, you will need to unpack some of the feelings you carry. At least they need to be named and owned. Those who interview you should be able to hear you out on these. Here are a few for your consideration:

Grief

All change has elements of loss in it. And all loss needs to be grieved. Name the loss that departure from the board may bring you. It may be the friendships you made—or the close working relationship with a pastor. You may experience loss of power or visibility in the congregation.

Anger

The root of anger is powerlessness—not being in control of events that affect us. You may have had the proverbial rug pulled out from under you. Sometimes an outside event over which you had no control has negatively affected your board work. Several of the responses quoted near the beginning of this chapter begged to be unpacked, for anger reigned supreme! You do not have to destroy with your anger or seek revenge. Neither do you have to swallow it. Just name it. Release it. And seek God's healing on it.

Guilt

You may be asking yourself, "I wonder what would have happened if only I had. . . ." Guilt is sometimes rooted in a grave offense—in which case forgiveness needs to be requested: "Lord, have mercy." More often, guilt raises its head when we second guess ourselves. You may be doing a number of "instant replays" of former board moments. They also need to be released. The gospel is still good news!

Fear

Who will you be "on the other side of the stream" when you no longer
have a clear identity label: "board member"? We sometimes attach our
sense of being and value to a position. If you have come to define yourself solely by this position, you need to release that as well. Return to
your deeper and authentic identity as a child of God who is a disciple.
Again—it's the gospel!

Joy and Satisfaction

Spend as much time on the positive feelings as on the negative. You
should have plenty to celebrate besides the fact that you made it and
survived! Your celebrations may even occasion a prayer of thanks and
praise right there in the interview room!

Investing in a New Calling

What will you do next? Where will you go from here? Your exit interview will need to include a goodly portion of time for you to explore
your next calling. Your experience on the board taught you to invest
your time and energies in response to God's call, rather than your own
preference.

Some people are so exhausted from their service that they want and
need a "vacation" from church service. If you need to disengage for an
extended period of time, you should have some support and direction for
your rest. Retreat houses have directors who help people make purposeful and productive retreats, even if a great amount of time is given to
silence. A pastor, wise elder, or staff member specializing in spiritual
direction could provide a real service in an intentional ministry for those
of you who choose to go to the desert for a time.

If you choose to spend time in that desert, at least nail down a time
now with the interviewing group when you can get back together to
discuss your next calling. Newly retired people often say, "I am busier
than I ever was. I don't know how I ever had time to do my work."
Knowing that they are newly retired, others put the rush on them, inviting them to volunteer in various ways. They easily become overex-
tended, and retirement does not become what they hoped it would be. So

be on guard. You have had a wealth of experience on the council. The rush of invitations may come your way. You will need to be more careful than ever in what you say "yes" and "no" to. That's why prayerful consideration with this small group of trusted spiritual friends is so important.

Your transition should not be "out to pasture." At this stage you will be a vulnerable candidate for "dropout." Here's what I mean in a slightly different situation. When new members join the congregation, they come carrying certain expectations. If they do not begin to realize those expectations and if they have not become involved with a group or activity in the church within four months, they will step onto the dropout track and invest their energies elsewhere—maybe in family or recreation. It happens so fast that the church wakes up a year later asking, "Where are these people?"

The same phenomenon happens to church officers and members of committees that have required a high level of involvement (especially pastor-nominating committees). If something else in the church doesn't soon capture your interest and involvement, you will likely commit your energies elsewhere. The exit team may have some suggestions based on your demonstrated gifts and interests or on their perceptions of the needs in the church. Lean on them! Once you have been acknowledged as a church leader with spiritual wisdom, you cannot easily shake that identity. You continue to lead whether you intend to or not.

Advisory Possibilities

Some churches create a sort of board "alumni" group of people known for their wisdom who minister in special ways or advise when called upon. Others set up "mentoring" systems for new board members, matching former members with new members for support and guidance. Ongoing support structures could include:

Trainers for ministry. You have been involved in a variety of ways. An apprenticeship under a pastor or lay leaders could qualify you to train people to teach, pastor, counsel, guide, and resolve conflict.

Counsels of elders. This is in contrast to an official council of elders. Counsels may advise the pastor, meet to pray and discern elements of spiritual life, or listen to the people. How about that? A group in the church whose sole charge and mission is to listen to the people!

Adjunct staff. Old church-staffing models of large, full-time, clergy staffs are giving way to models with fewer clergy—complemented by part-time paid or volunteer staff members. A former board member could become an official part of the church staff, complete with job description, office, accountability lines, and place on the team. This could be for a contracted term.

Portfolio carrier. Some tasks in the church don't need a committee to plan and carry them out. One person with background, interest, and abilities could be assigned to do a particular task on behalf of the pastors or church officers. Lyle Schaller observes that there are three kinds of committees: planners, studiers, and doers. People fall into these categories according to their gifts. Free those who have these respective gifts to use them.

Action and response teams. In a church I formerly pastored, a group of retired men called themselves the Good Eggs. Most had served on the session. They met every other Thursday morning for breakfast and fellowship. During this time they scouted about to see where a need existed to which they might make a response. They had no basic organizational structure. They simply used their gifts of awareness and discernment to lead them into witness and service projects.

Service on a nonchurch board. Your training and experience may make you a prime candidate for ministry outside the church on another board. The quality of life on a church board that exhibits worshipful work would make a unique contribution to another board. Three other sectors of boards beckon: not-for-profit boards, for-profit boards, and public sector boards. We are currently embarking on research to determine the interrelation of the issues, agenda, and cultures among these to see how service on a board can be an arena for ministry for the committed church leader who has an openness for a "call" in that direction. Stay tuned.

These suggestions are certainly not exhaustive. Who knows how many ways the Holy Spirit may lead those of you who have an ear and eye for what God is up to in our world?

I would strongly recommend that a follow-up session be scheduled four months after your exit for purposes of check-up and review. Those four months can be viewed as a "decompression zone."

Ritual Closing

Some type of ritual for releasing you would be appropriate. A ritualized closure can enable both you and the remaining board members to act out and make visible what is happening. I often recommend to boards that they select some symbol that represents their covenant. The selection or construction of the symbol helps them define the covenant more clearly and test the validity of what they have agreed upon. The symbol can be used at the beginning of the group's life as a means by which each person makes a commitment to the group. It also can be used during the course of the group's life as a point of reference and recommitment. Now toward the end, that same symbol can be used as a way to disengage and say "good-bye." One group used a series of ropes tied together to depict their unity and purpose. As members exited their ropes were untied.

When we closed Project Base Church a few years back, we celebrated its life in a closure rite created around Kubler-Ross's stages of grief. Participants walked though the various stages of grief—denial, bargaining, anger, depression, and acceptance—by entering five different rooms labeled accordingly. In those rooms they conversed with "a host" about the stage at hand. As we approached the chapel for closing communion, a sign over the door read "acceptance." Here the host asked us to take off our shoes, for this was "holy ground"!

After his resurrection Jesus conducted a ritual of closure and reinvestment—a kind of exit interview—with the disciples over breakfast by the Sea of Galilee. He served up fish cooked over an open fire. During the interview, he repeatedly asked Peter if he loved him—three times to match Peter's three denials. Then Jesus charged him to feed the lambs, helping him refocus where his energies were to be invested.

Rituals may extend into the total congregational setting. You were set apart in a public ritual in the midst of the congregation. Now it can publicly thank you and bless you by word, handshake, pats on the back, or other visible demonstrations of affection and appreciation. The church may give you a gift—a powerful symbol in itself. You may be given the opportunity to witness publicly to the growth you have experienced.

Affirmation and Blessing

I continue to hold a high view of your ministry as laity. I am convinced that ministry will be born and lived out from the center of the church's life, right in the hearts of set apart lay leaders. You have been spiritually aware and have functioned as a faith community, bonded in love and God's truth. Your life together has created new life in the congregation, even as leaven acts upon the loaf. You have modeled a quality of life together that has been an example to the whole church—inspiring it to greater heights of witness. Now the glory belongs to God alone, who loves the church and places the Spirit within it. Your board has been inspired. Now it is an inspiring one!

I join my voice with the apostle Paul, who prayed with much affection for the elders and leaders of the Ephesian church:

> I pray that you may have the power to comprehend, with all the saints, what is the breadth and length and height and depth, and to know the love of Christ that surpasses knowledge, so that you may be filled with all the fullness of God.
>
> Now to him who by the power at work within us is able to accomplish abundantly far more than all we can ask or imagine, to him be glory in the church and in Christ Jesus to all generations, forever and ever. Amen (Ephesians 3:18–21).

Sample Meeting Agenda
First Presbyterian Church,
Brandon, Florida

December 1991

7:00 p.m.   **We Assemble in God's Name**

- Evening prayer
- We light the Christ candle
- We are called to order and service—an Advent hymn
- We offer our praise and thanksgiving
- A quorum is declared

7:20 p.m.   **We Celebrate Our Past**

- Clerk's report
    1. Approval of minutes:
    2. Communication and correspondence
    3. Session report—November
    4. Pastor's report—November
    5. Outstanding projects—action update
    6. Approval of November financial statement
- We offer our prayer of confession
- We hear the Good News

8:00 p.m.   **We Proclaim God's Word**

- We study the Word of God
  Subject: The Prophetic Role of the Church Officer
- We share an affirmation of faith

8:40 p.m.   **We Present Our Offering**

- Mission and outreach ministry
- Christian education ministry
- We dialogue with youth
- Commitment and stewardship ministry
- Member care ministry
- Worship and music ministry
- Administrative support ministry
- Planning and evaluation ministry
- We offer up concerns of the past (old business)
- We offer up concerns for the future (new business)

9:30 p.m.   **We Give Thanks to God**

- We offer thanks for God's presence in our ministry
- We offer our prayers of intercession
- We remember our fellow session members (prayer partners)

9:40 p.m.   **We Go Out in God's Name**

- Charge and benediction
- We share the peace of God with one another
- We adjourn to serve

Board Culture Indicators

	Not Apply	Never	Seldom	Frequently	Always

1. We are accountable to the board for the care of a designated group of people.

2. The pastor looks to us for our counsel in the decisions the pastor makes in running the church.

3. Each of us represents the concerns of a particular group in the church.

4. Board members owe each other favors and have favors due them that will be useful in accomplishing the goals of the board.

	Not Apply	Never	Seldom	Frequently	Always

5. The positions that each of us hold on the board give us such pride and satisfaction that we find it difficult to think of giving them up.

6. We each carry a responsibility to manage a particular area of the church's ministry.

7. It is extremely important for our board to see all of the statistical indicators rise and grow.

8. We have a long-range plan before us and know exactly where we are in relation to it.

9. It is very important for us to conduct our business in strict parliamentary order.

10. Our greatest satisfaction comes from serving others,

	Not Apply	Never	Seldom	Frequently	Always

seeing ourselves
as stewards who
hold the mission
of the church in
trust for God and
for the people of
God.

11. Our meetings
have the character
of worship in
which we offer to
God our life and
work together.

Identifying Natural Leadership— Set Apart Lay Leaders Project

To whom would you look or go?	On the Board	In the Congregation
1. To fill you in on the history of the church or for background information on an issue?		
2. To assist you in bringing your vision into reality?		
3. To provide comic relief when a meeting gets tense?		
4. To pray with you over a specific concern?		
5. To figure out a difficult problem in the church?		
6. To encourage you if you were discouraged?		
7. To explore the biblical or theological insights on an issue or ministry?		
8. To assist you in resolving an interpersonal conflict?		
9. To listen to you when you want to talk and think out loud?		
10. [Other . . .]		

Chapter 1

1. Presbyterian Research Services, *A Study of Elders' Experiences on Session* (Louisville: Presbyterian Church USA, 1994), 21, table 19.

2. Dietrich Bonhoeffer, *Life Together* (New York: Harper & Row, 1954), 26.

3. Tilden Edwards, *Living in the Presence* (San Francisco: Harper & Row, 1987), 104.

Chapter 3

1. Author interview with Dr. Richard Chait, University of Maryland, June 1991.

2. James Hopewell, *Congregations, Stories and Structures* (Philadelphia: Fortress, 1987).

3. Author interview with Dr. Carl Dudley, 1991.

4. Author interview with Duncan MacIntosh, American Baptist Convention, Valley Forge, Pa., 1991.

5. Presbyterian Research Services, *A Study of Elders' Experiences on Session* (Louisville: Presbyterian Church USA, 1994), 11, table 9.

6. Ibid., 12, table 10.

Chapter 4

1. James Hopewell, *Congregations, Stories, and Structures* (Philadelphia: Fortress, 1987).

2. Walter Wink, *The Bible in Human Transformation* (Philadelphia: Fortress, 1973).

3. Robert J. Schreiter, *Constructing Local Theologies* (Maryknoll, N.Y.: Orbis, 1993).

4. Tom Sine, *Wild Hope* (Dallas: Word, 1991), 209-224.

5. Conway Associates, *The Reluctant Steward* (P.O. Box 3464, Louisville, KY 40201: Conway Associates, 1992).

Chapter 5

1. Archdiocese of Milwaukee, *Living the Spirit* (Roman Catholic Archdiocese of Milwaukee, 1991), 50.

2. Danny E. Morris, *Yearning to Know God's Will* (Grand Rapids: Zondervan, 1991).

3. Tilden Edwards, *Living in the Presence* (San Francisco: Harper & Row, 1987), 105.

4. Morris, *Yearning to Know God's Will,* 131.

5. Ibid., 135.

6. Wayne Purintun, "The Practice of Faithful Listening," mimeographed (Cincinnati Presbytery, 1323 Myrtle Ave., Cincinnati, OH 5206-1789). Drawn and adapted from a series, *Studies in the Spirituality of Jesuits,* 3 (September 1971), 4 (November 1972), 5 (October 1973); (St. Louis: Seminar on Jesuit Spirituality).

Chapter 6

1. Parker Palmer, *The Active Life: Wisdom for Work, Creativity, and Caring* (San Francisco: Harper & Row, 1990), 39–53, 74–77.

Chapter 7

1. Marliss Rogers, "Organizing and Sustaining Committee Life," *Action Information* 15, no. 5 (September–October 1989):20.

2. Eugene H. Peterson, *Working the Angles* (Grand Rapids: Eerdmans, 1987), 18.

3. Presbyterian Research Services, *A Study of Elders' Experiences on Session* (Louisville: Presbyterian Church USA, 1994), 4, table 2.

4. Ibid., 9, table 7.

Chapter 8

1. William A. Barry and William J. Connoly, *The Practice of Spiritual Direction* (San Francisco: Harper & Row, 1989), 194-95.

2. J. Oswald Sanders, *Spiritual Leadership* (Chicago: Moody Press, 1967), 20.

3. Reuben Job and Norman Shawchuck, *A Guide to Prayer for Ministers and Other Servants* (Nashville: Upper Room, 1983), appendix.

4. Presbyterian Church USA General Assembly, *Growing in the Life of Christian Faith* (Louisville: Presbyterian Church USA, 1989), 12-13.

5. Presbyterian Research Services, *A Study of Elders' Experiences on Session* (Louisville: Presbyterian Church USA, 1994), 6, table 3.

Chapter 9

1. Presbyterian Research Services, *A Study of Elders' Experiences on Session* (Louisville: Presbyterian Church USA, 1994), Q-30.

2. Presbyterian Research Services, *Presbyterian Panel Survey* (Louisville: Presbyterian Church USA, April 1982).

3. Charles M. Olsen, *Cultivating Religious Growth Groups* (Philadelphia: Westminster, 1984).

4. Dietrich Bonhoeffer, *Life Together* (New York: Harper & Row, 1954), 23-29.

Chapter 10

1. Pat Knutson (Overland Park Lutheran Church, Overland Park, Kansas) to author, June 6, 1994.

2. James R. Belt (Underwood Presbyterian Church, Omaha) to author, March 1989.

3. Michael Beaugh, "Report for the Set Apart Lay Leaders '94 Collegium," 1994.

4. Bishop Jack Wyatt, "Search Committee Formation," *Congregations*, 1994.

Chapter 11

1. Presbyterian Research Services, *A Study of Elders' Experiences on Session* (Louisville: Presbyterian Church USA, 1994), Q-30.

2. Ibid., 21, table 19.

3. Ibid., 19.

4. Ibid., 14, table 12.

5. Ibid., 20, table 18.

BIBLIOGRAPHY

Archdiocese of Milwaukee. *Living the Spirit: A Parish Council Manual.* P.O. Box 07912, Milwaukee, WI 53207, 1991.

Carloss, Susan. *Building an Effective Congregational Council.* Minneapolis: Augsburg/Fortress, 1992.

Hawkins, Thomas R. *Building God's People: A Workbook for Empowering Servant Leaders.* Discipleship Resources, P.O. Box 189, Nashville, TN 37202, 1990.

Lemler, James B. *Trustee Education and the Congregational Board: A Reflection on Leadership in the Community of Faith.* Trustee Leadership Development, 719 Indiana Ave., Suite 370, Indianapolis, IN 46202, 1993.

McKinney, Mary Benet, O.S.B. *Sharing Wisdom: A Process for Group Decision Making.* Allen, Tex.: Tabor, 1987.

Morris, Danny. *Yearning to Know God's Will: A Workbook for Discerning God's Guidance for Your Life.* Grand Rapids: Zondervan, 1991.

Morseth, Ellen, B.V.M. *Call to Leadership: Transforming the Local Church, Parish Council Formation/Education Session.* Kansas City, Mo.: Sheed and Ward, 1993.

Rademacher, William, with Marliss Rogers. *The New Practical Guide for Parish Councils.* Mystic, Conn.: Twenty-Third, 1989.